OREGON

THEN & NOW

HISTORICAL LANDSCAPE PHOTOGRAPHY BY
BENJAMIN GIFFORD

CONTEMPORARY REPHOTOGRAPHY BY
STEVE TERRILL

GIFFORD BIOGRAPHY BY THOMAS ROBINSON

AFTERWORD BY JOHN DANIEL

WESTCLIFFE PUBLISHERS

www.westcliffepublishers.com

CONTENTS

❖ ❖ ❖ ❖ ❖

TEXT

PREFACE, STEVE TERRILL
Standing in the Shadows of Benjamin Gifford   2

BIOGRAPHY, THOMAS ROBINSON
Benjamin Gifford, 1859–1936   5

AFTERWORD, JOHN DANIEL
Homing In on Oregon   187

❖ ❖ ❖ ❖ ❖

PHOTOGRAPHS

Oregon Coast   16

Portland   38

Willamette Valley   60

Columbia River Gorge   82

Cascades and Eastern Oregon   124

Southern Oregon   164

B ack in 1999—in the last century—I was contacted by Westcliffe Publishers regarding the possibility of undertaking this photographic project. As Linda Doyle explained the project in great detail, all I was thinking about at the time was the opportunity to publish another book. The challenge was to select a prolific photographer who had captured Oregon near the turn of the century, then rephotograph (as closely as possible) the same scenes to show the changes that had occurred over the past hundred years.

I jumped at the opportunity, believing this would be a somewhat easy assignment. I thought, how hard could it really be? I've traveled throughout Oregon for many years and I *thought* I knew most of my state. How could I have been so wrong?! You've heard of finding a needle in a haystack. I didn't have to locate just one needle—I had to find more than a hundred needles. The needles were Benjamin Gifford's tripod locations, and they ended up being scattered throughout Oregon with some in the most common locations and others almost completely obscured due to development or acts of nature. Fortunately, I had the assistance of my son Steve.

Let me start at the beginning. Upon accepting this *easy* project, the first step was to select a photographer whom I could follow throughout Oregon. I really needed help in finding the right one, and the Oregon Historical Society seemed a likely starting point. Just as I had hoped, they provided the names of a few photographers to start with and said I was welcome to look through their photographic files. Because I'm not well versed in most of the photographers' work, I needed help from an expert on the subject. This is when Tom Robinson's name came into play.

Tom is one of the top experts on Oregon photographers and is well versed in the field of photographic history, from the photographers to the printing processes. We met a few years back when we both had work in the same gallery. If I could get him interested in this project, I knew we would make a great team and produce an unforgettable book. Tom showed great interest in the project and agreed to work on it. Soon, we were off on an extraordinary journey.

Tom set out on the first task: compiling the names of Oregon photographers and profiling each one to help me select the perfect individual to "shadow." Tom and I narrowed the list down to four

STANDING IN THE SHADOWS OF BENJAMIN GIFFORD

By Gifford's Shadow, a.k.a. Steve Terrill

photographers, then after discussing all of them and considering the coverage and file/photo availability, we selected Benjamin Gifford. So the fun begins.

Our game plan was to review every photograph that had passed through Gifford's camera—no matter what condition they were in, from great to poor, we wanted them all. The starting point was the Oregon Historical Society. As Tom began the tedious task of poring through the files, he invited me to join in on the "fun." My job consisted of reviewing Gifford's works as Tom uncovered them and selecting the "keepers." As the hours turned into days and the days into weeks, I began to realize what a huge undertaking we had on our hands. At that point, we had viewed only a few hundred images and not even started to look into the private collections that held prints, negatives, and postcards.

One of the first challenges we encountered was locating all the Gifford negatives in the Oregon Historical Society files. Although most of Gifford's approximately 10,000 plates were still organized as a group, some of the best ones had been renumbered and mixed in with the Society's general files, which consisted of three million images. Thirty to fifty years ago, long-gone staff and volunteers had invented several different approaches to integrating Gifford's negatives into the Society's photo numbering system. Tom spent many weeks examining every large glass plate in the vaults to round up the Giffords that had strayed from the flock over the last half century.

Fortunately, Tom knew exactly what he was looking for as he painstakingly combed through the endless files. He was familiar with Gifford's style and numbering system, and he could recognize Gifford's handwriting at a glance—boy, was I ever impressed!

After a few weeks of reviewing files, we settled on a dozen or so images to get the book started. The game plan was for me to go out into the field and start shadowing Gifford to see if we were on the right track. I selected the Columbia River Gorge as my first victim. Let me rephrase that. The Columbia River Gorge was the first spot, of many, that victimized me. I lived close to the Columbia River Gorge, so I'd photographed the area for quite a few years. It seemed like a great location to get my feet wet. Heading up the gorge, knowing this was my first test, I felt an almost eerie sickness come over me. I knew approximately where Gifford had taken most of the photographs, but could the locations where he once stood change that much over the past century?

Approaching the first scene, my palms felt clammy and my heart started to pound harder. I was truly a nervous wreck. I decided I'd better put this panic into perspective before I started the book. After all, I wasn't out to capture a bald eagle soaring through a rainbow arched above a waterfall with Mt. Hood as a backdrop. No! I just needed to find a location and shoot from the exact spot Gifford did many years ago.

That's when the problem sank into my thick skull. For years, I'd been preaching the same philosophy to friends, family, and anyone who would listen: If you want to become a photographer, you should *never* copy another photographer's work—especially if you want to make a name for yourself in this business. Great. So much for "practice what you preach." I rationalized this break with the philosophy I had espoused so many times; I wasn't trying to *copy* Gifford or outrace him in hopes of publishing the images first. He had already beaten me to the publisher by about a hundred years! I needed to get over this hurdle of guilt as soon as possible for the sake of my sanity and the integrity of the project.

After resolving my philosophical issues, I arrived at my destination and was somewhat taken aback. I was standing near the camera position where Gifford had stood nearly a century ago. I was quite surprised and pleased to see that not much had really changed; the road was abandoned, the retaining wall had been reworked, and where moss once graced the concrete rails — as one might expect these days — graffiti had taken its place. All in all, the view still looked remarkably similar to the original historic photograph. I located the exact camera position, set up my camera, and began the technical part of rephotographing.

Then, without warning, I was slapped with another problem: my equipment! I had temporarily forgotten about the camera and lenses used in Gifford's days. The focal lengths I owned were not exactly the same as the ones used nearly a century ago, so I couldn't capture a perfect duplicate of the scene. Fortunately, I recalled conversations about this dilemma with Westcliffe publishers. We had all decided the book would be a pictorial history rather than a true rephotographic book that used photographic equipment from the same era. The project was simply intended to show the people of Oregon the major and minor changes that had occurred over the past century. If a view was blocked, I even had the option of moving slightly from the original spot to capture the majority of the image.

So with all this fresh in my mind, I hoped to photograph this first scene, get the film back, study the scene, and decipher where I had gone wrong. I received the sheets of film the next day, and I must admit I was somewhat pleased with the results. After critiquing every image, I realized I needed to be just a little higher and a smidgen closer to document the scene. This was the fine-tuning information I was looking for and needed in order to photograph the numerous vistas that lay before me. The race/challenge was about to begin.

Over the next few months, Tom turned over every stone, looked around every corner, and called in every favor in his quest for every possible image to review. Reviewing the images was tough enough. But then we had to narrow the field down to approximately 300 top choices in hopes that I could photograph half of them in a year.

Eventually, I started to feel overwhelmed. How on earth could I fulfill my contract in this period of time without help from an assistant in the field? Fortunately, a major player came into the picture. My crunch-time person who always came through for me — my son, Steve. After I had explained the project, Steve actually seemed more excited than I was. There was only one concern, and his name was

Stihl. Steve's dog, a bad-to-the-bone looking rottweiler, is a gentle dog that loves to play and interact with all types of people and animals. Stihl, whose name was derived from a chain saw, has a particular talent for clearing blocked areas. On command, he chews through branches and trees, or he clamps his vise-grip jaws on fallen trees and drags them out of the way as if they are fetching sticks. We weren't sure if Stihl was up for the journey, but we were going to give it our best shot. This was my "dream team." I was in the driver's seat and in charge of photographing, my son was riding shotgun and was responsible for scouting and assisting, and our muscle, Stihl, was in the back.

We began our journey in early April 1999. Throughout the year we crisscrossed Oregon numerous times, returning to some of the same areas on a few different occasions to capture the right perspective. An exemplary story comes to mind that I would like to share with you.

Traveling down I-5 toward Medford, I planned to stop at a few locations on the way. One of the destinations happened to be in and around the small town of Brownsville. Tom researched the vintage Gifford photos and believed at least two and possibly three images had been shot near the town. Pulling off the freeway, we began the task of locating these scenes, driving down paved and gravel roads and encountering dead ends from time to time. After several hours, we located two vantage points but had trouble locating the third.

We were puzzled, as it seemed like a relatively simple spot to find — two small buttes that diminished into a field of harvested grain. It had to be located north of the town; west of Brownsville the terrain consisted of flat farming fields, and the east was forested. After a few hours, we decided on a location, agreeing that the selected point was as close as it was ever going to be — or so we thought. The scene appeared to be the same, except for a few minor differences, but we expected that sort of thing. Unfortunately, the more we studied the spot, the more unsure we were of our decision. Maybe I needed to move back, or forward, or possibly to the side. Every move I made led to more confusion. I finally photographed the buttes, but I wasn't 100 percent thrilled with the shot and neither was my son.

Back on the road to Medford, we talked about the shoot in Brownsville and agreed that, during our trip home, we'd visit the area for yet another attempt to capture the image. A few days passed, and we found ourselves near the same spot once again, this time more determined to bag the shot for the book. While setting up my 4x5" camera, we noticed a truck heading down the road and thought this was our break. A local farmer had to know where the original photograph had been taken — or at least get us a little bit closer. Although he stopped out of curiosity, the farmer had only lived in the Willamette Valley for ten years and wasn't even sure if we were looking at the same buttes as in the Gifford print. That took the wind out of my sails! Tired from the trip to Medford, I decided to pack up and head for home, intending to return later and devote a full day to this image.

On the way home, I gave Tom a quick call and asked him to do a little more research on the image. It was really starting to bother me. Steve and I had located numerous locations we thought we'd never find, and this one seemed so simple. Tom agreed to do more research and promised some other possibilities within a few days. His research turned up a few interesting possibilities, which led us to other areas of the state. But by trial and error, the new spots were eliminated. So the road led back to Brownsville.

While traveling throughout the state and capturing other images for this book, the Brownsville shot was always in the back of my mind. The mysterious buttes became a challenge that ended up haunting Steve and me, even making Tom scratch his head a few times. Finally, we returned to Brownsville for the third time, determined to capture this elusive image come hell or high water!

We scouted north, south, east, and west for the better part of the morning. We even chatted with a few locals whose well-meaning attempts at help led us to some quite unbelievable dead ends. Tired and hungry, we decided to call it a morning and head to town for lunch. We spotted a small, quaint café, pulled over, and walked in to find that we had the place to ourselves. The waitress/owner was quite friendly, with that small-town charm I found so appealing. She didn't recognize us, so she asked what had brought us into town. My son explained the book project to her and took out the Gifford print in hopes that she would be our hero.

The waitress thought the buttes looked similar to the Washburn and Lone Pine Buttes north of town — two buttes we had already scouted. Kind enough to step outside and point toward the buttes, she was greeted by a dumb, bewildered stare from our protector, Stihl. She was amazed at the mild behavior of such a large dog and they soon became friends. The scraps of food and fresh water she supplied put a wag in his short tail; Stihl was living the high life. No matter where we went, from small town to large city, these types of people seemed to find us. Yet this town seemed to be a little friendlier than most — as we were soon to discover.

After leaving the café, we headed to the local grocery store to pick up some drinks, then headed out once again in search of our goal. As we neared the buttes from the south, Steve told me to pull over — he had an idea. Steve jumped out of the truck, held the print toward the sun, and instructed me to join him in this discovery. At first I didn't see what was so groundbreaking. Then he flipped the print and let the sun bask through the image — and it revealed the buttes that were before us! Wait, I thought, did Tom purposely print this backward to play a trick on us? I was about to find out. I called Tom, who said he would never pull such a dirty trick. But he explained why the photo might be printed backward: It was somewhat common in Gifford's era to flip an image for editorial purposes. I was pleased to hear his response, knowing we were finally on the right track. However, I wanted to eliminate all possible locations, so we checked out a half dozen other spots first.

Returning to the location where Steve had flipped the print, I was starting to set up my camera when I noticed Steve frantically searching for something. He scoured the ground and tore through the truck with panic on his face. I thought I'd forgotten the film or something worse. But it turned out that Steve couldn't find his wallet, which was full of a few new bank cards, checks, and quite a bit of cash. Thinking he must have dropped it at one of the other locations, we decided to forget about the photograph for now and look for the wallet. We backtracked to every location, but turned up empty. Steve knew he had his wallet at the café, but where else had we been? The grocery store! He figured we should forget about going back to the store; if he'd left it there, nobody would turn it in.

"Heck," he said, "I might as well buy a lottery ticket because the chances of winning have about the same odds."

But we did return. As we pulled into the parking lot, our eyes surveyed the ground with no success. I parked the truck and Steve headed into the store. I wish I'd had my camera ready to capture the ear-to-ear grin he was wearing when he emerged from the store with his wallet in hand. Not a thing in his wallet had been touched and the store refused a reward. I also went in to offer a reward, but the clerk kindly refused, explaining that the person who had turned it in didn't leave a name. I told the clerk about the book project and that I hoped to mention in the book the great people of Brownsville — from the café owner, to the honest folks at the store, to the lady at the meat smoker who gave Stihl a bone . I wanted to share these stories to illustrate that towns and people like this still exist. (And I for one hope they remain the same and are always a part of our culture.)

Leaving on a happy note, we returned to our photographic location and looked at the buttes in a different way. As the sun began to drop in the west and bathe the hills with a golden hue, our shadows stretched into the field like giants from a distant planet. As we finished our retake, we sighed with relief, believing we had won this round. Standing there, I reflected on the incredible experiences we'd already shared during this once-in-a-lifetime journey — and thought about what might lie ahead for us on this adventure. As we started to stow away our camera gear, a cloud crept past the sun, slowly diminishing our shadows as if they were melting back into nature. For some reason, my son and I watched our silhouettes until they disappeared. Without speaking a word, we took off toward our next "shadow" on this sometimes frustrating journey that we would nonetheless cherish forever!

This book is dedicated to my mother, Mary Terrill. Over the years, I've looked up to many people with great respect and admiration, but one towers above them all. Not only has she guided me through good times, but she has encouraged me through turbulent periods when it seemed that no one else cared. For that devotion I am honored to dedicate this book to her.

Benjamin Gifford (1859 – 1936)

Over the course of three decades, Benjamin Gifford produced more than 10,000 scenic and commercial photographs in Oregon. That number doesn't even begin to count his studio portraits. He was one of the state's most frequently published photographers during the first quarter of the twentieth century. A leader in the invention and development of what we now call the stock photography business, Gifford was the first Oregon photographer to operate a photo library stocked exclusively with images he had personally taken. Two photogravure books of his photography are, even to this day, the largest and highest quality photography books ever printed by an Oregon photographer.

Gifford's career wound through some of the most tumultuous years in the history of photography. He was a pioneer darkroom enlarger and mural printer, and his professional peak coincided with the decade in which photographic reproductions replaced hand-engravings in publishing. In addition, Gifford was a regional leader in photo postcard production.

Through these unpredictable times, Gifford's success was largely due to his skill in supplying pictures to publishers. The publishing experience, in turn, shaped his photographic style. Able to anticipate how his photographs would appear on a printed page, he used his camera to capture images that were published as panoramas, squares, and even in the round. Gifford realized that art directors would "crop" pictures to any size or shape that worked for their publication. Consequently, he used this knowledge to free himself of the slavery that standard print sizes imposed, and became the first Oregon photographer to completely abandon conventional proportions in his photography. Because Gifford anticipated custom cropping, his disregard for standard formats is a consideration when looking at the plates in this book.

Learning the Trade

Benjamin Gifford was born in Danville, Illinois. When he was twenty-one, his father sold the family farm where he had been raised, and Benjamin moved to Fort Scott to enroll in the Kansas Normal College. Here, he got his first photography job in a local photo studio. With two years of photographic experience under his belt, he moved to Sedalia, Missouri. In this city, Gifford spent the next two years

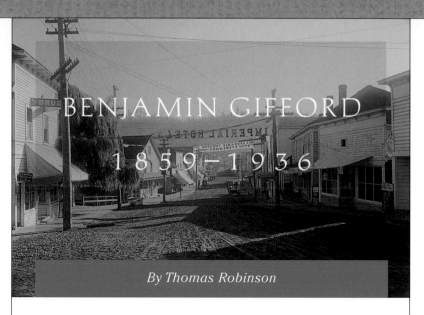

BENJAMIN GIFFORD
1859–1936

By Thomas Robinson

employed by William Latour, a former daguerreotypist who operated a prominent portrait gallery. Gifford later considered these four years of employment in portrait studios as an apprenticeship that taught him the photography trade.

Around 1885, Gifford returned to Fort Scott, Kansas, to form his first photography business, Tresslar & Gifford. His partner, Elkanah Tresslar, had been a photographer in Fort Scott for fifteen years. Gifford was replacing Elkanah's brother and departing partner, S.P. Tresslar. Their deluxe quality gallery graced a prime retail location on First and Main Streets. Tresslar and Gifford's portraits were handsomely embossed with their signature and mounted on gilt-edged cards. After two years, Gifford sold his share of the partnership. Around 1887, he set up a short-lived studio in Chetopa, Kansas, located on the state line of "Indian Territory," known today as Oklahoma. His Chetopa photographs were not as fancy as his big-city gallery work, but his photography skills in portraiture were clearly evident.

When Gifford moved to Portland, Oregon, from Kansas, he opened a photography studio at Sixth and Morrison Streets in a two-story building diagonally opposite from the Portland Hotel (where the Meier & Frank Department Store is today). In interviews with Gifford held thirty or forty years after the fact, he cited various years for his move to Oregon, which probably occurred in 1890. According to city and state business directories, a photographer

named Bushby operated the studio through the early part of 1890, William Hunt was the photographer through the latter part of 1890, and Gifford occupied it by early 1891, remaining there through 1893.

Gifford's earliest Portland photographs are imprinted with the Sixth and Morrison address; later ones switch to 313½ Morrison and one directory lists him at 115 Morrison. All these addresses are actually the same place. During 1891, Portland annexed East Portland and consolidated many other outlying communities. The post office alerted the city council that hundreds of streets had duplicate names; in one example, thirteen different streets all used the same name. Over the course of the fall, consultants produced at least three plans, and local newspapers published a number of other proposals. All the while, the address of every business in town was a speculative matter. After six months of debate failed to reach any sort of consensus, the fate of Portland's name and number system was finally resolved at a city council meeting during which members literally redrew the map. A department store window displayed the map the next morning and the newspaper wryly noted that everyone should see it "so you know where you live." Insurance company maps dating from the period show the Sixth and Morrison building as a photo studio, verify the address renumbering, and show no major changes in the studio structure from 1890 until the building was demolished shortly after 1900.

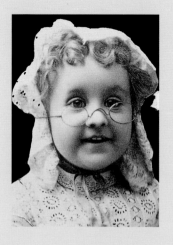

Gifford advertised his first photography business in Fort Scott, Kansas, by distributing this souvenir portrait as a sample of his work.

Gifford's studio (lower right), in a view taken after he moved out in the midst of the 1893 depression. Photographer O.S. Burns was the new tenant.

The studio roof held two hand-cranked dumbwaiters, each of which held a row of printing frames. In this ingenious arrangement, one row of prints could be exposed while the other one was reloaded. In the 1890s, photo prints were produced by sandwiching the printing paper and a glass negative in a wood frame, then exposing this to direct sunlight until the image "printed out." Each print was made individually, and because portrait sittings usually garnered an order for a dozen prints, the printing room could be a busy place. The brightness of the sun caused a variance ranging from three minutes to several hours in the time it took to make a print, so the weather determined the printing speed. With the glass hatch, Gifford could crank out customer print orders even during a rainstorm.

Gifford's studio sat half a block from the region's largest department store, across the street from the main post office, and diagonally across the street from the largest hotel in Portland. The trolley car line brought customers virtually to his doorstep, just as the MAX light rail system does today. The prime retail location explains why Gifford didn't advertise in newspapers, since his customers were walk-ins. An October 1891 newspaper classified offered the first-floor bakery in his building for sale as "one of the best locations in the city; good trade, cheap rent." The property improved in February 1892, when the muddy dirt street in front of his studio and its wood plank crosswalks were paved with asphalt for a fifteen-block stretch extending from the waterfront.

About two blocks east of the studio was the largest photo supply business between San Francisco and Seattle. The store was managed by George Weister, who later became one of Gifford's main rivals as Oregon's top scenic photographer. A block in the opposite direction was a patent medicine store operated by retired daguerreotypist Philip Castleman, a crusty old '49er who was a pioneer photographer during the gold rush days in many areas of southern Oregon and northern California. New emigrant Gifford likely got an earful of advice from these neighbors.

Gifford's early Portland portraits are identical to his Kansas work in many aspects. Rather than using the ornate backdrops and balustrades that clutter other photographers' portraiture, he opted for plain white backgrounds — a common denominator in all his early studio work from Missouri to Portland. Even Gifford's imprinted signature had barely evolved from the Kansas engravings; the distinctive Gifford signature that later became his trademark was years away. A photographer who produces such stylistically uniform portraits over the course of a decade, and halfway across a continent, might appear steadfast in his ways. But these similarities were actually a calculated effort to produce traditional, or classic, high-class portraits. To use the euphemism of his era, Gifford was an "up to date" man who posed with a conservative veneer.

Unfortunately, Gifford established himself at the very time that Oregon's economic trends spelled doom for his kind of studio. For one thing, Kodak's "you press the button and we do the rest" camera was cooling the market for frequent baby and family portraits. But it took the largest financial panic of the century, which struck Portland in mid-1893, to kill his Morrison Street studio. In the "Panic of '93," 20 percent of the American work force lost their jobs, 156 railroad companies were driven into receivership, and 400 banks failed. Gifford hung on through August 1893, but was gone by December.

Technology and Trends

Gifford's darkroom work during his first decade in photography is a study in contradictory intentions and results. Almost all of his pre-1895 portraits appear in reddish tones today. The true, original color of the prints was straight black & white, the exact hues of which you can see by examining the original, unfaded retouching on the prints. Because Gifford's wash time was insufficient, his prints faded to brown within their first few years.

This problem was by no means unique to Gifford; print fading has afflicted the entire photography industry since its beginning and, if anything, worsened as the twentieth century progressed. In the early 1890s, black & white prints faded to brown and led the public to think of brown prints as impermanent. The photography industry had the world believing photography could "secure the shadow 'ere the substance fades." Faded photographs belied that concept.

Gifford's initial response to fading was to extend his chemical immersion times and overtone his portraits to a deep black. After another few years, he realized his initial response was ineffective at preventing the erosion to lighter browns. Nevertheless, as we shall see, his efforts to study paper and processing paid off when he began to experiment with bromide paper.

A fortuitous confluence of factors bailed him out of financial failure in 1894. At this point in his career, his work began to mirror improvements and industry trends almost as soon as they appeared. Sometime between August and December 1893, Gifford moved out of his studio and began producing photographic enlargements in his home on Corbett Street. "I was the first photographer in Portland who ever made an enlargement of a photograph by electric light," he claimed. "In those days we had no daylight electric service. The electric light was not turned on until dusk, so I had to make all the enlargements at night." While his claim to be the first photographer to make enlargements by electric light is probably true, it is easily (and often) misunderstood. He is not saying he was the first to use electric light to take pictures in Portland—that distinction belongs to the Partridge Photo Studio in 1884. Gifford is also not saying he was the first to use electric light for making prints. Bromide developing-out papers, which were sensitive enough to be printed by electric light, had been available for about two years and were used by amateurs.

Gifford is specifically claiming that he was the first person in Portland to use an electric light bulb as the light source in what we now call an enlarger. The primitive enlargers in use back then were so different from what we use today that it's doubtful most photographers would even recognize them. Early enlargers, called solar cameras, were mounted on rooftops. They were designed to focus the sun's rays through a condenser lens, and had an astronomical mechanism to follow the sun across the sky. The enlargers needed this kind of light to expose the insensitive printing-out paper (POP) in general use then. Around 1892, a much more sensitive photographic printing paper entered the market. It was fundamentally different from POP for two reasons: It was a developing-out paper (DOP) and it was much more sensitive to light. All modern paper is DOP, which means it is exposed but no image becomes visible until it is chemically developed (that is to say, the image is latent until processing). The paper was not a big success in the market because professional photographers needed to remodel their darkrooms and retrain their work forces in order to use it. It was simply easier to continue to use the older system for the few enlarging jobs the average studio was called to do.

Gifford took advantage of the opportunity to become a wholesale producer of enlargements. By virtue of his idea and a darkroom built for his specific enlarging setup, he found a unique niche in the market—life-size prints (as they were called back then).

By luck or design, the timing of the depression that drove Gifford's studio out of business was ultimately advantageous to him for several reasons. First, Gifford could buy his paper stock for far less than it sold for only months earlier. Prices dropped for four reasons: (1) Manufacturer inventories of perishable photo materials in general and DOP stocks in particular were too high going into the depression, (2) the depression slackened demand, (3) Eastman Kodak's photo paper patents collapsed in 1894, and (4) paper manufacturers were in the middle of a vigorous price war. Second, Gifford was able to work at home while his son Ralph, born in July 1894, was an infant. Third, in the fall of 1894, a young photographer named Herbert Hale joined Gifford to form a new partnership called Gifford and Hale.

Pairing Landscapes with Enlargements
Herbert Hale, about thirty-two years old, was born and raised in Vermont. He spent the late 1880s as a photographer in San Diego

*One of Gifford's first photographs from his studio in **The Dalles**. Gifford's use of an ordinary rapid rectilinear type lens rather than the high-quality optics to which he soon upgraded for his landscape work caused the lack of clarity around the picture's perimeter.*

and spent 1890 in Downey. He moved to Portland on Christmas Eve of 1891 and landed a photography job at B.C. Towne's portrait studio downtown. In addition to portraiture, Towne sold scenic views of Oregon and Alaska. The side business worked well for portrait studios with printers on staff, as it filled lulls in the printing department's workload. Towne even placed an advertisement in Portland's 1893 city directory that consisted of an actual photograph of Alaska tipped in to each copy. This is the only edition of the directory to ever feature such an advertisement. While working with Towne, Hale likely noticed the way a gallery could augment its income by selling landscape views.

During the spring of 1894, Hale left Towne's gallery and set out on his own, becoming what we now call a freelance photographer. For Hale, that meant bicycling around the dirt roads of Portland's east side where he lived and drumming up whatever business he could. Hale carried his tripod and $6\frac{1}{2}$ x $8\frac{1}{2}$" plate camera on his bike and took pictures of families posing in their yards. Through a number of train and sternwheeler trips, he amassed a series of scenic views showing Oregon's most picturesque spots. In June 1894, when the largest flood of the century inundated 250 blocks of Portland with the overflowing waters of the Willamette, Hale captured dozens of shots of boats floating through downtown's business district. By the end of the summer, he was wholesaling a full line of his own scenic and flood views.

At this point, Hale formed a partnership with Gifford. The two opened a studio on the east side of SW Third Street (between Alder and Morrison Streets) and stayed for three years. Chances are, they remodeled the building into a photo studio from scratch. There is no record of a photography studio occupying the building before, although after they left it went through a succession of other photographers over the next ten years. Hale also moved his home to Portland's west side near Gifford's.

In the mid-1890s, dozens of photographers were competing on a wholesale basis to sell photographs of Oregon scenes. In downtown Portland, merchants stocked thousands of images. The ordinary landscape format, generally a small 5x8" boudoir-size contact print, had changed little since its introduction in the late 1870s. As a scenic view format, they were as generic then as the 8x10" print is today,

and they were mass-produced by studio printing departments, often with little care. Competition among the numerous producers and vendors, Hale being one of them, kept the prices low.

Gifford and Hale's partnership was unique among regional studios because it joined a landscape photographer with a mural printer. They briefly enjoyed a near monopoly on locally produced large-format scenic prints. Previously, large-format prints and murals had been special-order items among regional photographers, who were accustomed to sending their work to San Francisco for enlargement. The shipping charges alone made them expensive, and the risk of breaking an original negative during shipment, or the need for retouching, meant they usually had to send a copy. The reduced clarity resulting from a copy negative rendered the finished piece with a relatively flat tonal scale. Gifford's ability to enlarge

> **Gifford and Hale's partnership was unique among regional studios because it joined a landscape photographer with a mural printer.**

Hale's original negatives to mural size and control the entire process in-house gave the Gifford and Hale partnership a huge advantage. Not only were their enlarged prints much more profitable than the small ones, but Gifford was a master printer whose craftsmanship and careful printing transformed Hale's scenic photography into artwork worthy of framing.

Immersed in Landscapes

We can only speculate why Gifford left the partnership and moved to The Dalles in 1897, but it is likely that he was simply more ambitious than Hale. Certainly, Gifford was a more mature, knowledgeable, and experienced photographer and businessman. Looking at Gifford's and Hale's individual accomplishments over the next few years is a good indication of why they split. Hale downsized into a smaller studio and hired people to run it. His strongest works consisted of maritime views taken in Portland's harbor, but even those were not nearly as good as the harbor views routinely exhibited by members of the Oregon Camera Club. Gifford's accomplishments, by comparison,

speak for themselves. In three short years, he transformed himself into one of the state's most respected landscape photographers. No doubt motivated by Hale, Gifford dove into scenic photography. Although not entirely inexperienced with using a camera outdoors, Gifford had no opportunity for field photography during his early years in Oregon. His portrait studios were full-time jobs that had to be operated during daylight hours, and the business of enlarging photographs took up his evenings.

Although Gifford had done scenic photography years earlier in Kansas, the fundamental process of photography had drastically changed since then. When he learned photography, a camera was tethered to its darkroom. Shooting outdoor views meant bringing along an entire wagonload of equipment including a light-proof tent for making negatives. As Gifford later recalled, "When I first became interested in photography, the process was much more complicated. Dry plates were just beginning to come in, but the old-time photographers were doubtful of them. When we went out to take scenic views or pictures away from the gallery, we had to carry all our equipment with us. In those days our plate (negative) was a plain piece of glass. You held the plate in one hand, poured collodion over it, and then immersed it in a silver bath. You exposed the plate while it was still wet, and had to develop it at once, before it got dry."

After the Gifford and Hale partnership dissolved, sometime in 1897 Gifford moved from Portland to The Dalles. The date is shrouded in mystery because The Dalles newspaper is lost for these years and the fact was not reported in Portland newspapers. The only available evidence is the date of December 10, 1897, on a federal copyright registration for his photograph number 147 of a "Native with dug out canoe, Celilo, Columbia River." The return address on the application is Benjamin Gifford, The Dalles, Oregon. His early photographs from The Dalles, as a body of work, show Gifford's repeated efforts to capture dramatic views of the state's most often requested locations, as well as Indian portraiture and views of steamships on the Columbia River. Gifford later commented, "Atmospheric conditions are an absolutely essential thing in true photography.... The actual work consumes much less than five minutes, but the waiting for the favorable atmospheric conditions cannot be computed." Although he sometimes added clouds from

This 1906 photograph is an outstanding example of stop-action photography. The 1,400 kegs of powder blew 50,000 tons of earth from a basalt formation in the Columbia River Gorge. Engineers were building a railroad line on the north bank of the river across from Eighteen Mile Island, between Mosier and Hood River, and they considered this the greatest displacement of earth ever planned by humankind. The photograph was taken on a glass-plate negative, which was less than one-fourth as sensitive as the slowest color film available today. What makes this photograph particularly remarkable is the extremely low light Gifford had to work with. With sunset already past and the cliff deep in shadow, Gifford no doubt had to modify his plate development to get this image to come out. "Benjamin Gifford, who had gone from The Dalles to photograph the unique spectacle, saw the sun drop behind the mountains before the word was ready to 'let 'er go.' At exactly 6:20 o'clock the powder exploded; the camera performed its work in the ninetieth part of a second." (This means the shutter speed was 1/90. Gifford's aperture was at its probable maximum of F6.8.) The men in the photograph were a bit over 300 feet from the explosion and Gifford may have been around 400 feet away. It is amazing that his plate didn't break and the camera shake didn't blur his tack-sharp image.

other negatives to fill bald skies in his prints, his point is true. The common denominator in all his early scenic work is that it was suitable for mural-size enlargements to be displayed in train stations, and almost all the views could be seen by passengers on trains.

At this point, Gifford had equipped himself specifically for landscape photography with a set of lenses that used the new German formulas. Judging by the results, he had top-of-the-line Dagor- and Protar-type lenses. One undated newspaper clipping mentions that Gifford's camera cost $600 — the best available at the time. Gifford invested in lenses that allowed for excellent clarity on the edges of pictures as well as in the center; still a good test for lens quality today, this process sorts out inexpensive point-and-shoots from serious cameras. Of course, it is possible to get good edge definition from inexpensive lenses, but it requires the photographer to use small apertures. Because Gifford was photographing outdoors, small apertures presented an unacceptable compromise. Small apertures required long exposure and caused subjects such as tree branches, boats, and waterfalls to blur. At the time, most other photographers used far less expensive lenses; for small prints, and if the subject was relatively motionless and in the middle of the picture, it didn't really matter. Gifford's stop-action photography of sternwheelers on the Columbia River, taken in the days when it had rapids, shows the water splashing — frozen in mid-air — and tack-sharp across the entire plate. This was a genuine accomplishment for a photographer before 1905.

Gifford was a commercial photographer, so his interest in photography was pecuniary. His most artistic photographs are about specific subjects that he treated artistically, rather than art for art's sake. Although he ignored art photography per se, his photographic style emulated representational art. Around 1907, a newspaper review of an early Gifford exhibition effused, "There is something besides mere photographic perfection in these pictures. They breathe the very spirit of the outdoors, and each one is not only a reproduction of a scene, but a carefully composed picture. This is where the artist shows. There is one [*Sunset on the Columbia*]… which is truly a gem of composition and would have made a painter who could have imagined it a famous man." Gifford was indeed a genius in constructing outstanding photographic visions of scenic illustration. His work from 1898 to 1907 is among the most well realized portrayals of Oregon subjects ever made. Gifford's photography clearly describes the subject without drawing attention to his photographic technique. His compositions were rich and bold without the excessive nuances that characterized art photography at the time.

Gifford's work was also affected by his wife's health. He married Myrtle Louise in 1884, when she was twenty-one, and they had a son ten years later in 1894. By 1900, Myrtle had chronic health problems that required constant medical treatment. In 1902, newspapers mentioned her extended convalescent trips to other locations, sometimes lasting months. Her health never did improve; when she died in 1919, her obituary remarked that she had been a "patient sufferer and hopeless invalid" for "the past 18 years." Not only was Gifford constantly faced with expensive medical treatments for his wife, but he also raised his son, maintained his household, and was supportive to his disabled wife.

In The Dalles, Gifford's portrait studio and darkroom were on the Chapman block, later known as the Vogt block, on East Second Street (presently the site of a JC Penney parking lot). At this studio, he hired a staff colorist, Violet Kent, to hand-color the enlargements. She worked for him until she moved to New York in 1906. By this time, Gifford had resolved the darkroom problems that had caused prints to fade by extending his wash times. His prints made after 1900 faded very little — a century has elapsed and the photographic images still match the vintage retouching closely. Thereafter, he advertised "Gifford Photos Never Fade."

For bread and butter, Gifford circulated a traveling wagon and tent studio throughout the Inland Empire. He advertised it as "The finest photographic studio ever put on the road." As one newspaper noted, "While at Hood River last Friday we called at Gifford's traveling studio and found the genial and successful artist up to his ears in work. He has fitted up the studio with the latest and only sky-light of the kind in the northwest, backgrounds, and everything up-to-date." Legend has it that Gifford preferred to take his scenic photographs in the spring before the seasonal forest fires darkened the sky every summer, but it's also likely that his tent studio was on the

Sunset on the Columbia. Gifford's most famous photo is known variously as *Sunset on the Columbia* or *Wa-Ne-Ka*, an Indian name Gifford translated as the "halo of the evening sun." Its original title was *Home Guard* and, later, it was *Teepees on the Columbia.* "I believe it is the most artistic picture I had ever taken," Gifford said. On the way to photograph sheep, he spotted the scene bathed in "subterranean light." The photograph's location is actually in Washington, near present-day Maryhill. After developing the picture, Gifford added clouds from another negative. The photograph became famous almost immediately and many stories of its making were later published. Not surprisingly, the tales behind the photograph became somewhat mythological.

All accounts of the photograph's origins agree on one point—the Indians did not want to be disturbed or photographed and they refused to pose. After Gifford took this photograph, one Indian threw rocks at him, successfully driving him off. Historians have given various dates for this photograph, but it was certainly taken before 1901.

road as early as possible every spring because the first itinerant photographer to visit a small community would get the lion's share of customers wanting their portraits taken. Even today, photographers prefer Oregon's relatively mild spring temperatures to the film-melting heat of August.

Microfilms of The Dalles newspaper are blank for the first three years Gifford operated his business there, but they pick up again in 1901 just in time to announce his preparations to permanently leave The Dalles and move to Portland on May 1. *The Oregonian* reported that Gifford, along with another darkroom mural printer and an art gallery owner, were forming a corporation called the Portland Art Company. The article named Gifford as

the company's photographer and enumerated his better-known photographs and the fame they achieved. Although the company never got off the ground, and Gifford did not actually move to Portland from The Dalles, the gist of both the Portland and The Dalles newspaper items about Gifford in 1901–1902 indicate he had earned a reputation "back east" in the four years that he had been in The Dalles.

Years later, Gifford described showing his photography to A.L. Craig, the general passenger agent for the Oregon Railway & Navigation Co. railroad (which ultimately became Union Pacific). He told Craig, "A few hundred pictures like these, scattered out in the east, will do more to bring farmers and settlers to Oregon than all the books you can print." Gifford got a job with the railroad and became one of the primary suppliers of photo murals to the railroad industry for display in train stations. "For years I finished enlarged photographs of scenic and farm views to the railroad companies," he claimed. The railroad job explains how a small-town photographer became famous throughout the nation in such a short period of time. In the early 1900s, trains were the only practical form of long-distance travel; each city's depot was functionally similar to an airport of today. From coast to coast, the waiting rooms of these terminals were decorated with beautiful photo murals bearing Gifford's stylish signature. This incredible feat of self-promotion single-handedly elevated his name recognition into international status. The story also explains the beginnings of his relationship with the railroad industry, which, as we shall see, became his most important photography customer later in his career.

By 1902, the railroads were already relying on Gifford for photography. A newspaper item from February 26, 1902, noted, "B.A. Gifford says a person must get a move on himself to keep up with that jumping jack of an industrial agent, Judson. Yesterday morning he received word that Judson's special car would pass through town in fifteen minutes and for him to be ready to go up the road and do some work for them. Mr. Gifford found it impossible to get his paraphernalia ready on such short notice, so the train was held a little time, and off they went for Willows....Mr. Gifford took a number of views at different points along the road to be used by the company in advertising."

Gifford later recalled, "I became tremendously interested in the scenic Columbia River. I was the first person to get out an album of Columbia river views which I called 'Snapshots of the Columbia.'" Gifford's federal copyright application for the book, printed by photogravure, was granted on October 2, 1902.

The Lewis & Clark Centennial Exposition
The year 1905 was a big one for Portland, host of the Lewis & Clark Centennial Exposition. This was the first world's fair held in the United States west of the Mississippi, and its effect on the local economy can hardly be underestimated. The fair attracted 1.5 million visitors and the influx enriched practically everyone. The event's

immediate economic effect on Gifford was not substantial, but it did end up benefiting his photography. One factor in the delayed impact was Gifford's remote location, ninety miles away from Portland in The Dalles. Gifford was also hurt by the fair's official policy that prevented him from photographing it. Until Lewis & Clark, most fairs in the United States charged photographers daily fees of about $3 per day for camera and tripod permits. This antagonized amateurs, but was actually a plus for a professional like Gifford, who would just as soon clear the clutter of amateurs out of his way. However, a young rival of Gifford's, Fred Kiser, who had worked the 1904 St. Louis fair, trumped all the other photographers by signing an exclusive contract with the Lewis & Clark fair to be its official photographer. In exchange for a royalty on the official photographs, the fair banned all other photographers (although handheld snapshot cameras that produced only small negatives were permitted). The fact that no other photographer could use a tripod on the fairgrounds prevented Gifford from shooting any pictures at the fair. He might have been able to come up with a creative workaround, but his style

An example of the Rembrandt-style lighting Gifford used in his later Indian portraits.

was so deeply ingrained with the use of traditional tools—a view camera and 8x10" glass plates—that he didn't.

> *Gifford routinely traveled through Indian reservations on his winding route to small towns with his tent studio. The high-demand subject matter would be ideal for mural-size enlargements, of which he had become the top printer in Oregon.*

Gifford did do a reasonable amount of self-promotion work for the fair, including publishing a set of his Columbia River photographs that he marketed as a quasi Lewis & Clark souvenir. The high-quality photogravure reprints from his 1902 book were suitable for framing, and the inexpensive packaging as loose prints in simple printed envelopes lowered the price enough to sell them in drugstores.

Another factor of the Lewis & Clark fair that stimulated Gifford's development was his exposure to one of Edward Curtis' first international-class exhibitions of American Indian portraiture. Although Curtis had been published by several eastern magazines, he was still relatively new and unknown at the time. Curtis started photographing Indians about the same time Gifford began his landscapes. Gifford no doubt saw the exhibit and read with interest the newspaper review explaining that Curtis "has exchanged ease, comfort, home life, for the hardest kind of work; frequent and long-continued separation from his family; the wearing toil of travel through difficult regions, and finally the heart breaking struggle of winning over to his purpose primitive men." The newspaper noted that Curtis "pays gold to each individual for the privilege of pointing the dreaded camera toward them. He has been known to travel with a group of Indians for hundreds of miles to find the proper backing—the right landscape—for a characteristic picture."

Within the next two years, Gifford made his most famous Indian photographs using precisely the techniques described in the Curtis review. Gifford routinely traveled through Indian reservations on his winding route to small towns with his tent studio. The high-demand subject matter would be ideal for mural-size enlargements, of which he had become the top printer in Oregon. Plus, Gifford had about twenty-five years' experience as a portrait photographer. Although he had been taking Indian portraits for years, the Lewis & Clark fair marked a change in Gifford's style of photographing Indians. For his new studio work with Indians, Gifford brought out dark backgrounds and used Rembrandt-style lighting.

Making New Markets

Along with the 1905 fair, several factors contributed to the creation of new markets for Gifford's style of photography: the improved mechanical printing of photographs, a railroad war, and, most important, the professionalization of regional development. The San Francisco earthquake and fire forced West Coast publications such as *Sunset* and *Pacific Monthly* to rebuild their printing facilities from scratch; within six months the magazines rebuilt with all-new presses that yielded distinctly better photo printing quality.

The competition among railroads racing to build lines through every state makes little sense today, but at the time no one could have foreseen how automobiles would ultimately ruin the railroads' dominance of transportation. Capitalists viewed each line as an eternal money-minting franchise. Following the completion of the transcontinental lines in the early 1880s, the emphasis in railroad development shifted to trunk lines. For railroads to remain profitable, additional passenger and agricultural freight traffic was essential. The railroad industry's only option was to create demand by attracting settlers. Railroad corporations, in concert with government programs, earnestly sponsored what later turned out to be one of the largest resettlement programs in the history of the human race. To accomplish its goals, the program offered special emigration fares and free land for permanent settlers (homesteading). Railroads and local commercial clubs (boosters) split the promotional work. Boosting had long been practiced by local politicians and land speculators, but by 1905 professional advertising agencies overtook local efforts. The active help and capital of railroad lines enabled the lavish printing of emigration pamphlets. And the brochures featured writing by professionals with imaginations far more fertile than the land they were promoting; extolling a region of limitless opportunity, the articles verged on motivational therapy.

Of course, the statistics citing Oregon as an international leader in lumber, flour, and wheat production were real. Portland was the largest city in the Northwest and was doubling in size again. Portland manufactured more lumber than any city in the world, and Oregon's forests held one-sixth of the timber in the United States. But if there was any doubt about the writers' portrayal of Oregon as a hubbub of commerce and success, then it fell upon the photographer to prove the point. Because so many of the potential emigrants had limited reading skills, either due to poor schooling or because English was not their native language, the emphasis on professional photography became particularly critical.

Magazines such as *Sunset* showcased the new professionalism of boosters. Before 1905, most of the photographs were made by the writers themselves, or the writers selected works of obscure amateurs or local studios. Because the photographers were flattered by national publication, their shots usually cost the magazine little. Although a good source for simple scenes, these photographers were out of their league when it came to complex subjects. Views of urban streets featuring tall buildings and zooming traffic required equipment that amateurs couldn't afford and didn't know how to

Fruit Propaganda. *The natural appearance belies a carefully arranged advertising production. It would be difficult to imagine a scene more ripe for photographing.*

use. The stylistic differences between the products of a landscape artist and those of a commercial photographer worked in Gifford's favor at this time. Landscape photographers traditionally used a meditative spin to convert virgin nature into visual poetry. Editors of development periodicals wanted photos to suggest the pleasing effects scenery could have on people who took trips for pure enjoyment. A commercial photographer, for example, usually included people and cars in a landscape's foreground.

Gifford's work debuted in *Sunset* magazine in the October 1905 issue. The magazine's "Columbia's Crags and Castles" article featured photography by Weister, Kiser, and Gifford—commercial photographers who were rivals for the next twenty years. Ironically, Gifford was the oldest, but his photography career outlasted both Weister's and Kiser's. Weister died in 1922. When Kiser's studio failed, he moved to Los Angeles and penned a self-help book titled *The Hidden Power of Money*.

The Hood River area serves as a classic example of the effectiveness of professional boosting. In 1902, Hood River apples wholesaled locally to shippers for 50¢ to 80¢ per box. By 1910, the price had jumped to more than $2. In addition to agricultural improvements, the primary factors that drove the price up included promotional advertising and packaging. As land prices soared, overalls gave way to Prince Alberts, and the Hood River Commercial Club became nearly as powerful as local government. The fruit propaganda industry became a core business in the community, especially when the locally produced and nationally distributed *Better Fruit* magazine began publication in 1906. Gifford's studio was uniquely prepared to furnish *Better Fruit*'s color cover and numerous illustrations.

As the publishing of railroad booklets became centralized in Portland, another market expanded for Gifford. The "Sunset Commutative Plan" offered 55,000 booklets to prospective cities for $1,200. The frenzy of communities to attract settlers can hardly be underestimated—for example, in Mosier, the newspaper noted that "they raised $1,210 in a few minutes for publicity." Through photography, communities attracted more people and raised the value of their property. For example, Gifford photographed the Fleck Orchard near his studio for The Dalles Business Men's

Immigration pamphlet. *Gifford took photographs for the Medford Commercial Club (organized in 1906), which produced a new booklet annually and sent hundreds of thousands of them to eastern cities. By 1911, Medford trebled its population, quintupled its business, and octupled its property values.*

Association, which featured his photos prominently in booster pamphlets. When Fleck initially cleared and planted his hillside homestead, locals literally laughed at his choice of grapes as a crop. In 1908, he sold his orchard for $60,000 and it was sold again in 1910 for over $100,000.

The economic value of quality photography was readily apparent, but the artistic demands of black & white agricultural photography were little understood. Despite numerous attempts, more than twenty years elapsed before a photographer of Gifford's caliber would again produce photographs of comparable graphic composition in the area. Agriculture photography is primarily used for illustration in publications. Gifford was also a specialist in making hand-colored photo murals, and it took sixty years before anyone in the area approached his success with large-format colored photographs.

A paradox of stock photography is that it can be used to illustrate any aspect of a subject. One notable example appeared in a 1908 magazine article by C.E.S. Wood, a highly regarded Oregon author and artist. Wood brilliantly captioned a photograph that Gifford initially made to promote logging. The springboard portrait of axe-wielding loggers was captioned, "The dollar rules, and except for the Government reservations there has been no thought of preserving a specimen of what mysterious Nature was a thousand years in building into infinite beauty." Wood elaborated about the splendor of the falling forests: "It is a pity to have all this majesty of antiquity wholly destroyed. Man cannot restore it. It cannot be rebuilt by Nature herself in less than a thousand years, nor indeed ever."

The Postcard Renaissance

When a 1907 act of Congress changed postal regulations to make sending picture postcards more practical, Gifford found another market for his photographs. Picture postcards were not new, but senders were not allowed to write a message on the address side of the card prior to 1907. The congressional act divided the back of the card into a correspondence section (on the left) and a mailing section for the address, postage, and cancellation (on the right). For the first time, if a photograph covered the entire front of the card, the sender could still write a message on the back.

The golden age of the postcard was born—an era that lasted until about World War I. The fad kicked in right away and postcard sales skyrocketed. In the fiscal year after the new postal regulations kicked in, post office figures show, 677,777,798 postcards were mailed in the United States. According to postmarks on old cards, Gifford got in the game and started the wholesale manufacture of postcards no later than March 1908. At first he relied on printing presses to lithograph the cards, but by 1909 he was making actual photographic cards, commonly known today as real-photo postcards.

Concentrating on the Corporate

Gifford's career peaked in 1909. First, he was commissioned to photograph Neahkahnie Mountain for real estate developer Simeon G. Reed, who published the prints in an impressive large-format book. More significantly, Gifford published an enormous folio-size book of his own photography, titled *Art Works of the State of Oregon*. The extremely high-quality photogravure reproductions, with tissue interleaving, comprise the largest and best-printed Oregon photography book ever published. In May, Earl's Court in London exhibited Gifford's hand-colored Columbia River photographs, enlarged to mural size. During the summer, Gifford also found time to photograph numerous city and county booster booklets.

At this point, Gifford's work had evolved into managing a photography business. In the most important change since he founded his studio in The Dalles, he now used his camera exclusively to fulfill photography contracts. Although he was still taking his own pictures in the field, Gifford had long ceased operating portrait sittings himself. The spring tours through small towns were gone with the horse-and-buggy days, and he now spent summers traveling with railroad and development promoters or as the guest of business associations.

Gifford's summer hosts were flattered by more than his fame. Gifford understood—better than almost all his contemporaries—how to invent attractive identities for communities through photography. His photography was the perfect antidote to the pervasive image of the Wild West that Buffalo Bill Cody had introduced to easterners thirty years earlier. Gifford merchandised it as a tame West. His shots of meticulous orchards, with rows of crops arranged in geometric precision, spoke more effectively than a thousand real estate agents.

By 1909, railroad companies (which were investing massive amounts of money promoting travel and emigration) and real-estate developers had become Gifford's prime customers. A new publishing trend emerged at this time, which turned out to be a windfall for Gifford. In their promotional booklets, publishers started to print more photographs than text, and they used four-color presses for the cover as well as the inside plates. The lavish printing quality was novel and impressive. Among all of Oregon's photographers, Gifford was uniquely prepared to furnish this type of artwork because he had the largest and best file of colored photographs. His decade-long investment in colored photographs enabled him to enter yet another new market as a master. (In July 1909, *The Dalles Chronicle* carried an account of Violet Kent, a Gifford staff colorist for seven years. While working for Gifford, Kent had saved enough money to pay for art school at the Pratt Institute of Brookings, New York. She was graduating, with honors, from a four-year art course in only three years.)

The Push for Portland

By the end of March 1909, the west winds of the Columbia Gorge had dried the rain-soaked roads of The Dalles sufficiently for Gifford to drive his spoke-wheel "buzz wagon" (car) around town. Good roads and bridges were practically nonexistent in Wasco County. Throughout most of the state, drivers could operate autos only during the summer, so Oregonians took long-distance trips by train. Gifford certainly spent that summer living in Pullman cars and hotels, regrouping at his base of operations when he could. He turned forty-nine in August, and at the end of this grueling summer returned home to The Dalles. Here, Gifford discovered that the city reservoir was empty and the engineer was going to shut off the city's water.

Although the main street was scheduled to be paved, the town featured a new hotel, and the number of street lights had increased from twenty-two to thirty-three, the location in The Dalles was a decided disadvantage for a busy photo studio aspiring to national markets. Gifford needed to be in direct and daily contact with the engraving and printing companies in Portland. At the very least, he needed passable streets for driving and water for his darkroom. Just as his father had done thirty years earlier, Gifford literally sold the farm. The Giffords sold their Union Street home, which sat on top of the bluff overlooking The Dalles. In addition, Gifford sold his photo studio to its longtime manager, Charlie Lamb. The newspaper didn't record the transaction, and later accounts by Gifford, Lamb, and other sources cite various years for it, but the date Gifford, his wife, and son moved to Portland was noted by *The Dalles Chronicle* as May 31, 1910.

Gifford frequently returned to The Dalles to take photographs in the area. Statistics show that during the first six months of 1910, between 53,000 and 55,000 emigrants settled in the Northwest. Because the downtown sections of most western towns were either recently built, rebuilt, or in fact construction projects, similar sized towns had similar appearances. As a result, competitive communities relied on Gifford's photography to emphasize the unique advantages of each location. So when planning the 1910 promotional booklet, The Dalles' budget committee selected Gifford to make its photographs. When he arrived in June, *The Dalles Chronicle* noted that Gifford "has done more than any one other person to advertise The Dalles and the Columbia River valley." The *Chronicle* also published an account of a chance meeting between the secretary of The Dalles Business Men's Association and a lost and bewildered easterner seeking directions. "This sure is a barren looking place," said the traveler; "there surely can't be anything around here to support the city." The Dalles' lack of name recognition among easterners underscored its need for further self-promotion.

Operating from his new base in Portland, Gifford continued to expand his markets for enlarged murals of his photographs. By then, his work was gracing the walls of hotels and public buildings across the country. The public schools in Chicago, for example, ordered a set of his hand-colored enlarged photographs, and photography for railroad publications kept him busy as well. In 1912, Gifford published a second large-format book of Oregon photography, with tissue interleaved photogravure plates, titled *Art Works of Portland, Mt. Hood and the Columbia River.*

In the last six years of his career, Gifford continued taking photographs and administering his photography business. During this time he accomplished one significant body of work—documenting the construction of the Columbia River Highway. During the course of its construction, he became a personal friend of the highway designer, Samuel Lancaster; and he obtained a contract to make mural photographs of its progress for display at the 1915 world's fair, the Panama-Pacific Exposition.

It's somewhat difficult to attribute images from the last years of Gifford's career because he was relying on his staff of hired photographers as well as his son, Ralph Gifford (who joined the

Train wheels at the Union Pacific Yard in Albina, 1918. Taken by the Gifford and Prentiss studio with their extra-wide-format 7 x 11" camera. The specialized "banquet camera" format made negatives that reduced proportionally to postcard sizes.

navy in 1915). Exactly how many photographers he had on staff or who they were will probably never be known. With the ring of a phone, Gifford's studio was as prepared to photograph an automobile advertisement as an automobile accident.

Around this time, in one last effort to rejuvenate his business with fresh blood, Gifford formed a partnership with Arthur Prentiss. A commercial photographer interested in the same kind of scenic work Gifford did, Prentiss was actually a partner with George Weister—Gifford's chief rival for the preceding decade—from 1912 to 1916. The Gifford & Prentiss studio was in downtown Portland on Washington Street between 12th and 13th Streets; the partnership lasted less than two years. Later in his career, Prentiss became known for his daring mountaintop photography.

Gifford's Retirement

After nearly twenty years of a progressively disabling illness, Gifford's wife died on April 7, 1919. In August 1919, Gifford turned fifty-nine and officially retired. He then married Rachel Morgan, a former schoolteacher from The Dalles, on October 15. He had begun working closely with Morgan in 1913 when she became his staff colorist. The couple retired to a home Gifford built on Salmon Creek, about six miles north of Vancouver, Washington.

An undated newspaper clipping published shortly after his retirement mentioned that Gifford and his new wife were taking a trip to Imnaha and then to New Meadows. "For the first time in my life," he said, "I am starting off with absolutely no thought of taking pictures. I am going to hunt and fish, and where we are going there is the finest opportunity for that sport." Although Gifford maintained a studio in his new home, it's doubtful that he did much work there. But retired photographers seem to clutch their cameras until death pries them from their grasp. Apparently, he did continue to make large framed prints of his *Sunset on the Columbia*. Gifford delighted in telling his stories to interviewers, including his most widely quoted interview with Fred Lockley in 1928, and he posed for the Oregon Historical Society's first photographer, Frank Aldrich.

Gifford's son, Ralph, returned from his navy tour in 1919, then opened his own studio on the Mt. Hood Loop Highway at White River. Ralph continued to print from Gifford's negatives, using his father's distinctive signature on his own postcard photographs, which he sold through his studio until 1928.

Gifford passed away on March 5, 1936. Samuel Lancaster, a friend of Gifford's, delivered the eulogy and noted that "the Oregon country never had a better friend" than Benjamin Gifford.

Gifford's Negatives

Ralph Gifford sold most of Benjamin Gifford's library of stock photography to Sawyer's Scenic Photo in Portland. The company was interested in negatives suitable for printing postcards, which were actually copy negatives of large plate originals. Sawyer's erased Gifford's distinctive signature from the negatives and replaced it with "Sawyer's Scenic Photo." The whereabouts of the negatives is unknown.

Sawyer's also wound up with an enormous quantity of Gifford's original 8x10" plates. A May 1946 article in the *Oregonian* about Sawyer's Scenic Photo noted that the company had Gifford's collection in its vault. In a 1949 interview, Gifford's widow, Rachel, said Sawyer's had up to 12,000 of Gifford's large original negatives. These negatives are now at the Oregon Historical Society, where they have been since at least the mid-1960s.

When Ralph Gifford sold the main library to Sawyer's, the family removed and kept a number of plates and photographs. In 1986, these were donated to the Horner Museum in Corvallis. After the museum closed, the collection was transferred to the Oregon State University Archives in July 1996.

The portrait negatives Gifford's studio took in The Dalles are, according to numerous reports from old-timers in the area, gracing the windows of every greenhouse in Wasco and Hood River counties.

With no one to learn from, we read dozens of photography manuals from the 1880s through the 1920s, as well as ancient photography magazines, to unravel the theory and practice of using this material.

Printing Gifford's Negatives

The majority of the images in this book were printed from Gifford's original negatives from the collection of the Oregon Historical Society. To duplicate Gifford's results as closely as possible, the prints were made the same way Gifford himself made them, which is on printing-out paper, or POP (Ilford introduced the acronym POP in 1891). These photographic printing papers are the ancestors of today's darkroom papers, and are in fact gelatin chloride paper. Invented in the 1880s, POP became the standard printing paper for the photography industry for the next twenty years. Although Kodak discontinued the paper years ago, one small factory in England still makes it for museums and artist photographers who appreciate its particular qualities.

Glass negatives from a hundred years ago do not print well on modern papers. The tonal range of these negatives greatly exceeds the capacity that modern-day papers can handle. Old negatives have a very long density scale, designed to be printed on the type of paper manufactured back then. When attempting to print historic negatives on modern paper, the range of dark to light values quickly overruns the new paper's scale. The result is that the dark areas of the print "plug up" (the shadow areas all turn black) and the light areas "block up" (they simply don't print at all). Even the midtones are placed in the wrong part of the scale. Of course, there are a lot of darkroom procedures that can mitigate these problems, but you can easily spend days making repeated efforts to print a single negative before getting an excellent print. Even after going through all that work, you still won't produce the rich detail Gifford did because POP behaves in a fundamentally different manner than modern photographic processes. As you expose POP, the shadow areas darken normally at first, then become progressively less sensitive to light as the exposure continues; meanwhile the highlights continue to print normally. The effect is called "self-masking," and it gives POP a unique ability to interpret a negative's local contrast differently than its global contrast. Computers cannot duplicate the result because scanners today are unable to interpret such a long range of light to dark values, and no software exists that can emulate the self-masking effect.

To make the prints for this book, we brought Gifford's negatives up to the roof of the Historical Society, which is located only four blocks from Gifford's original studio in Portland. Using antique printing frames that were over a hundred years old, we exposed the paper by sunlight without electricity. We often joked with the digital photography technicians that our darkroom was ready to change centuries in either direction.

Reconstructing long-obsolete photography procedures is in itself challenging. With no one to learn from, we read dozens of photography manuals from the 1880s through the 1920s, as well as ancient photography magazines, to unravel the theory and practice of using this material. Much of the early literature about techniques and chemical formulas was variant, if not contradictory, and it took dozens of attempts before the entire process could be debugged and controlled to the point of consistent results. The substantial amount of trial and error was, however, worthwhile in order to learn the fine points of the medium, and information from the old photography magazines was useful in understanding Gifford's evolution as a photographer.

Astoria, *Hammond's Mill,* before 1909

Sewage Treatment Plant, April 1999

Andrew Hammond got his start working in logging camps around Pennsylvania. He then migrated westward, stopping in St. Louis to work on riverboats, then arrived in Montana where he opened a store that later became the Missoula Mercantile Co. This profitable enterprise enabled Hammond to invest in building a railway. He then moved to Oregon and in 1894 bought the Yaquina railroad. In 1898, Hammond organized this lumber mill in Astoria (which burned down around 1930). He was considered one of the first to turn out finished products from a logging mill instead of selling raw lumber. With the fortune Hammond accumulated, he was able to form a consolidation that bought much of California's redwood forests.

In Gifford's time, logging and fishing activities occupied Astoria's waterfront. Today, a different sort of industrial activity transpires on the Columbia River shoreline. The camera location was adjacent to a nearly completed residential construction project.

Astoria, before 1909

April 1999

This photograph was originally published in Gifford's Art Works of Portland, Mt. Hood and the Columbia River *as "Decapitated Forest Monarchs Ready For The Miller's Saw."*

The miller's saw is gone today and the supply of forest monarchs has been depleted. As we were photographing, neighborhood children played next to us on the shore, and they were probably having just as much fun as when Gifford was photographing this spot.

Cannon Beach, *Third and Spruce Streets,* summer 1917

Built around 1903, this structure's original name was the Hotel Bill. In 1910, the hotel was renamed the Cannon Beach Hotel and it became the official post office for Cannon Beach. License plates on the cars and the seasonal foliage help date Gifford's photo, indicating that it was taken shortly after the United States entered World War I in April 1917. Woodrow Wilson was the hotel's most famous guest.

After the Cannon Beach Hotel was demolished in 1971, the Cannon Beach Christian Conference Center was built on the site (at Third and Spruce Streets just south of Ecola Creek). Many of the quaint log cabins in Cannon Beach have given way to the concrete of development.

Chapman's Point, *Clatsop Beach,* before 1909

Gifford published this photograph in 1909 in his Art Works of the State of Oregon.

Since the trail to this lookout washed out a few years ago, this section is nearly inaccessible. The safest way to reach the point is to hike down a steep hillside near the park's office. Sliding part of the way, we reached the location and headed back just in time to miss a torrential downpour.

Cannon Beach, *Hug Point Looking North,* circa 1897–1918

To reach this point, we needed low tide and a break in the weather. We were rained out a number of days, but on the final day we returned, we lucked out. The only problem was that just about everyone else near Hug Point decided to visit the waterfalls that day. You can't see them, but standing behind me were a number of people kind enough to wait until we finished our retake.

Manzanita from Neahkahnie Mountain, 1909

Gifford didn't have the luxury of automobile roads to climb the mountain; he had to use the old Indian trails that led to the top.

I took this photograph from one of several roadside automobile pullouts on the highway that crosses the west facade of the mountain. Because this is usually a quite windy spot, I was fortunate to be here on the calmest day I've seen here—the tree limbs are not blurred by the wind's turbulent movement.

Manzanita from Neahkahnie Mountain, 1909

September 1999

After making one failed attempt to locate Gifford's shot, we returned in a month to try again. One hundred years of shore erosion and real estate development made locating Gifford's vantage point a confusing and bewildering proposition.

Newport, *Nye Beach, Jump Off Joe,* 1910–1913

Newport, *Nye Beach, Yaquina Head Lighthouse,* December 1999

The rock formation dubbed Jump Off Joe, a well-known tourist attraction in the years before World War I, was subject to rapid erosion. Returning visitors always made it a point to check on its changes since their last visit. In the 1880s, the rock was connected to the cliffs on the mainland, presenting a 100-foot-high obstacle to beach travel. Early settlers named the spot Jump Off Joe because travelers would have to climb up one side and then jump to slide down the other side to get past it. This changed when natural forces separated it from the mainland in the 1890s.

Gifford's view was taken around 1910–1913, when the monolith had eroded to a shadow of its former size and the beach had become a passable roadway. The scene delighted several generations of amateur photographers, who endlessly snapped the lighthouse framed by the hole. Jump Off Joe collapsed during a severe storm in late January 1916.

Today, only a few rocks protrude from the sand at the site of one of Newport's most popular early twentieth-century attractions. Over the years, several similar geologic formations have come and gone along this part of the coast, but none as famous as the original Jump Off Joe.

Nehalem and Nehalem River, circa 1915

April 1999

When Gifford photographed Nehalem around 1915, it had its own newspaper, lodges, and commercial club. Boosters speculated that coal development would ignite the economy, but it was a bust. Today, the town remains about the same size as it was when Gifford photographed it.

The tree on the right obliterated Gifford's viewpoint, so we stepped over to a private residence for our vantage point. Because flooding occurs with some frequency in this riverside community, Nehalem has been raising the elevation of its business section to reduce flood damage.

Haystack Rock and Cape Kiwanda, circa 1909

Gifford took this photo from the beach west of Pacific City within a year or so of the city's founding and the establishment of its post office in 1909.

Lion's Head at Newport Beach, circa 1898

Gifford's son Ralph, born in July 1894, is featured in this photograph from around 1898. Lion's Head is on the right and the Yaquina Head lighthouse is in the background.

September 1999

During the course of the last century, winds obliterated the features that gave Lion's Head its name. When I took this picture, the wind was so gusty that my son had to hold the tripod down to prevent it from blowing over.

Marshfield, circa 1897–1918

This town was renamed Coos Bay shortly before World War II.

Coos Bay, September 1999

This photo illustrates some of the difficulties in rephotographing Gifford's negatives. Tom figured the location of the original shot was St. Helen's. Wrong. So we checked the neighboring city of Rainier. That didn't look too good either, so we stopped off at city hall to see if anyone knew where Gifford's shot was taken. The clerk said we should talk to the mayor, who was on duty at the tavern he owned across the street. The mayor said he didn't know where it was, but it wasn't in his town.

It was time to call Tom to clarify the identification. Fifteen minutes later, he called back and admitted making a 200-mile mistake. We bade good-bye to the mayor of Rainier and headed to the other end of the state. We arrived in Coos Bay the next morning and located Gifford's vantage point. Then we spent the day waiting for someone to come home so we could get permission to set up a camera on his or her property. At the end of the day, the owner appeared but could give us only a few minutes to make our shot.

35

North Bend, circa 1897–1918

September 1999

North Bend is located at the northern tip of the peninsula above the city of Coos Bay.

Gifford's vantage point is now blocked by a three-story concrete building. We made the best match we could from the access catwalk on the building's back, shooting at the end of the day to approximate Gifford's lighting.

Rockaway, circa 1915

December 1999

I shot this image under many different lighting conditions, but was still unhappy with the results. We returned a few weeks later and rephotographed this scene three more times. In a hurry to leave town, I left all my paperwork and prints on top of the truck. As we pulled out of town, they were scattered somewhere on Highway 101.

Portland, *Lewis & Clark Fairground,* circa 1905

One of Gifford's rivals, Fred Kiser, was the official photographer for the Lewis & Clark Centennial Exposition. Kiser had an exclusive contract with the fair that banned other photographers from using cameras with tripods. The ban prevented Gifford from using his bulky 8x10" view camera inside the fairgrounds, effectively prohibited all serious photography of the fair, and provoked public outrage. Despite editorials in the Oregon Journal *and the Oregon Camera Club's lobbying campaign, the ban was upheld. Gifford made this early morning overview of the fairgrounds from a nearby bluff, which is presently the site of Montgomery Park.*

Northwest Portland Industrial Area, September 1999

Photographed from the third floor of Montgomery Park's parking garage, this image captures the original site of the Lewis & Clark Fairgrounds. Shortly after the fair, most of the buildings were scrapped and none of the original structures from Gifford's photo remain today. Two structures were saved: the Forestry Building (which burned down in 1964) and the Royal Typewriter Building (which was moved to St. John's and recently renovated by the McMenamins for a brew pub).

Portland, Bird's-eye View from King's Heights, circa 1897–1918

September 1999

It was impossible to duplicate Gifford's shot due to urban growth. The only clear view I could get was from the foundation of a house that had recently burned down.

Mt. Hood and the City of Portland, after 1912

Portland, *Bird's-eye View from Pittock Mansion,* January 2000

Looking through an antique store, I happened to find this postcard (at left). I was on a constant lookout for Gifford postcards in hopes of finding one that was new to us. I did not remember this one, so I set out to rediscover Gifford's camera location. After searching for hours, I discovered he had shot the photograph from Pittock Mansion. This time, I surprised Tom with the postcard and the completed rephotography.

Portland, *Multnomah County Courthouse,* circa 1916

Construction on this courthouse, designed by architects Whidden and Lewis, started in 1909 and was completed in 1914. Whidden and Lewis also designed the neighboring Portland City Hall, the Arlington Club, and many of Portland's fine homes. An excellent neoclassic Roman building with inlaid marble floors and ionic columns, the courthouse was the largest building in Portland as well as the largest courthouse on the West Coast. Reflecting the demands of our litigious society, remodeling has doubled the number of courtrooms in the building since its construction.

I thought we should wait for a major holiday — when traffic would be moderate to light—to shoot some of the core images of downtown Portland. We set out on Christmas Day with a strange-looking camera and a mean-looking dog. Needless to say, we stuck out like a sore thumb! With the scare of the Y2K celebration just around the corner, two people, a security guard, and the police promptly questioned us.

Linnton, *Pacific Gas & Coke Co.,* circa 1915

Gifford shot this scene during the plant's final stages of construction. The plant is located on St. Helen's Boulevard about six miles northwest of Portland's city center. The Shell Oil refinery and the railroad bridge crossing the Willamette River sit in the background.

Pacific Gas & Electric Co. Building, November 1999

Although it was easy to locate this spot, the new growth obscured Gifford's original viewpoint. This shot, which includes NW St. Helen's Road, Route 30, had to await the winter. When Linnton was annexed to the city of Portland in 1913, Portland gained the largest wilderness park of any city in the United States.

Swan Island, circa 1911–1918

This photograph was labeled as Sauvie Island, but when we got there, one look told us the identification was probably wrong. Could the landscape have changed this dramatically over the century? After careful study of the picture, I detected a small bridge in the center that told me it was actually Swan Island. I shot this from an overlook at the University of Portland; the Port of Portland shipyard is below and the city of Portland is in the distance.

Portland, *SW Washington Street, 1911–1913*

Gifford shot this picture of SW Washington Street, looking east from 14th Street, from a fire escape on the old Carlton Hotel between 1911 and 1913. At the time, horse-drawn vehicles were still predominant in Portland. The Hotel Ansonia (at right) housed the original W.C. Winks Hardware store (the third door from the corner), which is flanked by the Fuji Co. Japanese imports shop and Louis Marks Jewelers. Over the next fifty years, Winks absorbed most of the first floor of the building. The hardware store finally moved in the early 1970s, when the building was demolished to make room for the freeway.

This view of SW Washington Street, looking east from 15th Avenue and Burnside Street, encompasses the 14th Avenue Bridge and the I-405 Underpass. It was impossible to duplicate Gifford's camera position because the building he photographed from has been replaced by a sunken freeway. Our only vantage point was the roof of the old Marquette Hotel. We weren't expecting the rooftop to be an expensive penthouse. I was surprised by how hard my son Steve had to push the heavy steel rooftop door to open it. With a mighty shove it opened and Steve was gone! He and my camera equipment landed in a pile on the rooftop landing below.

Portland, *6th Street,* circa 1919

December 1999

Looking north up 6th Street shortly after 1919, you'll see the Pioneer Courthouse on the far right. Gifford's original Portland studio was located on the site of the four-story building just past the courthouse. See the O.S. Burns Photo Studio, in the same spot, in the mid-1890s photograph on page 6.

This view, looking north at the intersection of Yamhill Street, is another Christmas Day shot. We hung around for an hour waiting for the sun to come around one of the buildings of this concrete jungle, and apparently started to look suspicious to the security guard, who questioned us. Even though it was Christmas, I still had to avoid the Tri-met buses cruising the transit mall.

Situated on the corner of Yamhill and Lownsdale (now 14th), The Mallory Hotel remained prominent in Portland throughout the entire century. Built around 1901 as an eight-story fireproof structure, it suffered only one major disaster—during the severe 1916 snowstorm, the sidewalk overhang collapsed. When a cocktail lounge was added to the hotel, some of the first-floor windows were bricked over.

Portland, *Washington Park,* circa 1897–1918

Created in 1891 by John (Hans) Staehli, this fountain is topped with a small cast-iron boy modeled after the artist's son. Staehli is best known for the cast-iron ornamentation that graced some of Portland's best nineteenth-century buildings — all of which have been razed.

September 1999

The cast-iron boy on top of Staehli's fountain, shown in Gifford's photo, has since disappeared.

This view of Portland from the Blitz-Weinhard building overlooks the streets of Tenth and West Burnside.

When retaking this shot from the Blitz-Weinhard building, brewery personnel were very helpful and allowed us to go anywhere. Unfortunately, our view was limited because the roof was a forest of industrial tanks. Our vantage point was an expanded metal grating on a high-voltage electrical hazard. We used ropes to lift the camera equipment up — to tie ourselves down because the breeze could easily blow us off the roof into the busy traffic below.

Portland, *SW Park Avenue and Madison Street,* prior to 1917

December 1999

You're looking north down the unpaved SW Park Avenue in this photo taken from its intersection with Madison Street. The buildings on the far right were demolished and the site is now home to the Oregon Historical Society, which is the custodian of Gifford's glass negatives. We made most of the prints for this book on the roof of the Oregon Historical Society's new building.

The worst part about taking this picture was finding a parking spot nearby. In desperation, I parked at the entrance to the Portland Art Museum and quickly set up my camera and tripod. When an official from the museum started eyeing my 1955 Chevy Nomad, my son intercepted him while I readied my plea for one shot. But the official turned out to be the museum's curator of photography, and we shared an interest in Benjamin Gifford, classic cars, Linhof cameras, and good coffee.

Linnton, *Willamette River,* circa 1908

Army Corps of Engineers, September 1999

Gifford published "On the Willamette at Linnton" as a photogravure in his 1909 book Art Works of the State of Oregon. *The location for this shot is very close to the Pacific Gas & Coke building shown on page 44, although Gifford took this picture about five years earlier.*

While exploring this property, now belonging to the Army Corps of Engineers, my son spotted Gifford's original camera position next to an army plant. We found the place where Gifford had set up his tripod between two maple trees and captured the shot.

St. John's, *Willard Tires,* after 1915

Lombard Flowers, December 1999

I attempted to capture this image four separate times, using a 4x5" camera, a 6x7" camera, and numerous lenses with both. Finally, I realized the problem: I needed to be in the exact middle of Lombard Street, which is a main thoroughfare. Once again, my son became my traffic director. To our surprise, a Portland officer greeted us with a friendly wave as he drove around my camera.

Clatskanie, after 1908

To match the lighting in the Gifford photograph as closely as possible, we visited this spot the day before taking the shot. During our visit, we realized that photographing in the middle of this busy intersection with a heavy tripod would be far more dangerous than it had been in Gifford's day. So when we returned the next day, my son and I wore bright orange vests to ward off the speeding log trucks, which seemed intent on converting my camera into a casualty. After a number of hurried attempts to focus the camera and expose the film, we finally captured it without getting killed.

Willamette River and Oswego Bridge, circa 1917

Gifford's image shows locals enjoying themselves by the riverside.

October 1999

We encountered a few dead ends while trying to locate this shot, so we were relieved to finally find Gifford's camera position. Unlike Gifford's shot, stairways now lead from the shoreline to the residences that line the river. One such staircase proved to be our best vantage point.

When a curious property owner asked what we were doing, we explained our photography project to him. He asked to borrow our working copy of the Gifford print so he could make a copy to show his neighbors. We were happy to lend him the photo, thinking he'd be gone for only a few minutes. After fifteen minutes had elapsed and he hadn't returned, we were wondering what to do — we needed the Gifford print to line up the rephotography. After an hour, with the light fading fast, we were concerned that our opportunity was evaporating. Eventually, he returned and asked if we were able to get the shot. Not realizing that we needed to use the work print, he had been driving around looking for a copy machine that could make a quality reproduction. He was very apologetic about the mixup, and we were able to use the remaining light to expose a nice 4x5" of this scene. In a sense, we felt as if our copy of the scene had taken nearly a hundred years to make.

Factory in Oregon City, circa 1897–1918

Sullivan Plant, May 1999

As in this case, one of the challenges of rephotography is obtaining permission. Initially, we were refused entrance to this highly secure mill. The manager finally allowed us to photograph the area, but he warned that if we took more than a few minutes we would be locked in the grounds overnight. Matching the lighting, beating his clock, and making our getaway required split-second timing. I must say, we made one of our fastest reshoots for the book on this day.

Oregon City, circa 1897–1918

May 1999

After searching the upper part of Oregon City, we finally found the closest possible spot to the original location — now a church parking lot. We backed our truck up to a fence (which was covered with poison oak) to create a good shooting platform, then I maneuvered atop the tailgate of the truck to avoid the shrub. Unfortunately, the wind was blowing enough to brush the nearby branches onto us, and a few days later we were both itching from that lovely plant!

Oregon City, *McLoughlin House,* after 1909

Built in 1846 by Oregon's founding father, John McLoughlin, this building was originally adjacent to Willamette Falls. In the early 1900s, a paper mill bought the land and wanted to move or demolish the decayed building. Preservationists, including photographer Joseph Buchtel, launched a campaign to save the historic structure. (Buchtel created the best-known portrait of McLoughlin — a daguerreotype taken in his Oregon City gallery shortly before McLoughlin's death in 1857.) The preservationists were successful, and the difficult move was completed in 1909. Gifford's photo shows the building after its move and restoration.

The community of New Era served as a railroad terminus on the Willamette River where ships could exchange loads without having to travel farther down to the falls near Oregon City. Gifford photographed this spot while on assignment for Sunset *magazine; the November 1910 article actually included a hand-colored view taken from a slightly different angle. The writer used the photograph—which showed the valley and farm below to better advantage, but omitted the figure that gives scale—to illustrate how agricultural cultivation transformed the Willamette Valley into "a paradise of peace and plenty."*

Rephotographing this spot was a trip back in time for me. While traveling to my grandparents' farm near Hubbard, my parents always told my brother and me to watch for the balanced rock on the cliff. On each journey, being the first to rediscover the rock became a competition for us. Tom Robinson reintroduced me to the pillar, but it was mislabeled as the Columbia Gorge. I laughed, then told him this childhood story, knowing quite well the actual location.

I finally had a reason to do something I've always wanted — scale the cliff to get a closer look. Bad move! The side of the cliff was steep and sprouting poison oak. My son, his dog, and I were covered with it. Oh, did I forget to mention the stinging nettles?

Orenco, after 1910

Orenco, *MAX Light Rail Car,* July 1999

Sixteen miles west of Portland and three miles east of Hillsboro, Orenco was established as a post office in 1908 when Oregon Electric Railway officials named the town and built a railroad siding there (at left). Orenco was named for the The Oregon Nursery Co., which established plantations in the area in 1867. By 1925, the company was the largest nursery in the Northwest, growing fruit trees, shade trees, shrubbery, vines, berries, and bulbs. The company town had a hotel, two confectioneries, and two general merchandise stores.

Silverton, after 1907

Main and Center Streets, July 1999

In the early 1900s, Silverton was in a decline. The Oregonian noted that "for several years…not a single new house had been erected in Silverton. The town was about as lively as a morgue." In 1907, investors formed The Silverton Lumber Company, which built a logging railroad that shipped out seventy cars of old-growth timber each day. The local payroll added more than $18,000 to the community each month. Overnight, Silverton paved its streets, businesses revived, and the town experienced tremendous municipal growth.

After the private timber tracts were clear-cut, in 1913 the company sold out to new investors, who expected to log federal lands and envisioned converting the already clear-cut lands to wheat and fruit orchards. The potential freight revenue from agriculture, combined with the needs of their logging mill, enticed the investors to buy Baldwin eight-wheel locomotives and upgrade the tracks, rather than use the Shay geared locomotives on the hair-raising ride typical of a logging railroad. At one end of the line lay 3 billion board feet of Douglas fir, and at the other end investors were building the largest log dump in Oregon to accommodate it. Silverton needed to attract people, so Gifford portrayed the community as a fine place to raise a family, rather than a logging town.

Over the years, the streets and sidewalks in Silverton were moved dramatically. I had always thought that in smaller towns, the roads stayed in the same place and were simply paved and improved — not moved.

Railroad Bridge at Troutdale, after 1910

6729

The fast current of the Sandy River at its lowest level indicated that Gifford took this shot in the summer. My son and I waded across the river as if we knew what we were doing, recorded the image, and proceeded back toward dry land. About halfway back, I spotted a shortcut and veered in that direction. But, as most people know, there is no such thing! Not only was I the last to cross the river, but the deeper water filled my boots with a quart or two of the ice-cold Sandy River. My son got a good laugh out of that one.

Crawfordsville, *John McKercher Mill,* circa 1897–1918

This community, which houses the John McKercher Mill, is approximately eight miles from Brownsville on the Calapooia River.

Old Swimming Hole, September 1999

With the mill gone, we were left shooting the "Old Swimming Hole" on the Calapooia River. As we were shooting this image, my son's dog, Stihl, romped along the water and chewed sticks. Suddenly, Stihl started barking, then charged toward us with terror in his eyes! Don't forget this is a rottweiler, widely regarded as a mean breed. Unless he had discovered a hornet or wasp nest, we couldn't figure out what the problem was. As we slowly walked back to the scene of the crime, Stihl started to bark nervously, and we spotted the problem. A stick was moving! Stihl did not know what to do with this curious stick, which just happened to be a snake.

Brownsville, *Bird's-eye View,* circa 1903–1906

Although a fire destroyed many of Brownsville's buildings in 1919, it remains one of the best-preserved towns in the Willamette Valley. Today, most of its buildings predate 1925, with some going back to the 1880s. "Brownsville is what it was," notes Don Ware, the editor of the town's newspaper.

Notice the building under construction at the bottom of this photograph. During one of our many return visits to Brownsville, we observed that the new building now blocks the view shown in this image. Lots of luck to the photographer in 2099 who might attempt to document the town from this location.

Brownsville Vicinity, circa 1903–1906

April 1999

Gifford made this picture during a photo shoot for a promotional booklet titled "How to Get to Brownsville Oregon," although this view was not used in the booklet. Amidst intense competition, railroads published booklets boasting the benefits of each community. This particular booklet, published around 1906 by Southern Pacific, provided specific train connections, times, and ticket prices from any major city in the United States. The house in the foreground was torn down about 1996.

After a two-hour search, we located the hill where Gifford took the original photo and the owner of the property graciously granted us permission to travel along an old farm road that led to the top. To our disbelief, the hill was covered with thickets of wild blackberry vines that towered well above our heads. The vines were so high that, when we reached the summit, we could not see to the valley below. To get the shot, we decided to upright some discarded, rusty fuel tanks to make a platform. The ends of the tanks were uneven, so it was quite difficult for me and my tripod to balance on them. My son tried to steady the tanks while handing up film for my shots. Gifford's original location was approximately fifty feet to the right and fifty feet down the hill.

Albany State Bank, May 1910

April 1999

This view captures the north side of First Avenue at the corner of Ellsworth. According to the calendar posted inside the bank, Gifford took this shot on Tuesday, May 24, 1910.

Eugene, before 1909

Gifford published this photograph in Art Works of the State of Oregon *as "The Picturesque Mill-Race at Eugene." The number 1903 in the lower right corner is Gifford's photograph number, not the date.*

My son and I were expecting to find this pond nestled on or near a farmer's field. When we became frustrated with our search along the waterway, we found a few people from the University of Oregon to help us locate Gifford's spot, which turned out to be on the campus.

Multnomah Falls in Winter, before 1910

February 1999

Multnomah Falls is Oregon's most popular tourist destination. After the original bridge collapsed in 1910, the falls went without one until Benson Bridge was installed in 1914.

Multnomah Falls, circa 1917

March 2000

Although I really wanted this image in the book, I was understandably hesitant to stand in the middle of a train trestle with only my son to warn me of speeding locomotives heading toward us. Once, while looking through my 4x5" camera with a dark cloth over my head, we heard the whistle of an approaching train and scampered to safety. People were watching us as if we were stupid, crazy, or both. Despite this stress, we captured the shot without causing a big train wreck. No doubt, Gifford experienced similar risky moments while taking his photographs a hundred years ago. In these situations, the secret to success is to quit while you're ahead. I'm sorry about the black & white, but the color shot will have to wait for another century!

Shepperd's Dell Bridge, *Old Columbia River Highway,* circa 1917

To stay out of traffic on this curved road, we stood as close as possible to the basalt cliff that hugged the side. While we were waiting for the lighting to improve, many passing vehicles nearly clipped us or the camera equipment, and it wasn't long before an Oregon State Police officer arrived. Dreading an expensive ticket—or worse—I explained the project and showed him the work print of Gifford's shot. The officer was very understanding and even helped direct traffic while I made the photograph.

Also known as the Needles, the Pillars of Hercules takes teamwork to photograph. You need two people with wide-awake eyes to watch for oncoming trains, each continuously covering a different direction. I credit my life to my son and one of his friends on this day—I got this shot with only seconds to spare!

Pillars of Hercules, circa 1897–1918

This shot of Pillars of Hercules is from the confluence of the NPRR tracks, I-84, and the Columbia River. Looking out over this scene, we were intrigued by the major removal of the smaller rock monoliths that once graced the Columbia River at this location.

Bishop's Cap, circa 1915

During this retake, I wondered how many people who approach this part of the highway are unaware of the rock formation hidden behind the forest. You can still see Bishop's Cap from the other direction, but it doesn't have the same impact as this approaching view.

Viaduct on Old Columbia River Highway, after 1915

Gifford shot this view of the viaduct on the Old Columbia River Highway at Cascade Divide between Bonneville and Eagle Creek.

This spot presented a major problem — height! The truck was not allowed on this road; but even if it had been, we wouldn't have been able to position it properly for use as a shooting platform at the necessary elevation. I discovered that I could get close to the correct height by standing on the concrete rail surrounding the viewpoint, but my tripod still didn't extend high enough. I had to call every camera store in Portland to find a tripod that extended eight or nine feet. We picked up the tripod and headed back the next day to capture this image.

Multnomah Lodge and Columbia River Highway, 1917

Built around 1915, Multnomah Lodge was at the base of Mist Falls and about 400 feet west of Wakena Falls. The lodge changed its name to Mist Falls Lodge around 1920 and a business card advertised that it "can accommodate a limited number for weekend parties. Breakfast, lunch, and afternoon teas at all hours. Oregon Products Featured. Long Distance Phone." The lodge burned down around 1929 and only the old stone fireplace remains.

Site of Mist Falls Lodge, April 1999

When I first became a photographer in the 1980s, I stumbled on this area in the gorge. Ever since, I've been puzzled by the chimney standing near the road with no building in sight. Finally, it all came together when I saw the Gifford print and discovered that the lodge had burned down. This is a great example of how nature slowly heals itself.

I was anxious to reshoot this image because it shows the constantly changing landscape of this gorge. As recently as the winter of 1987, part of the cliff broke off and fell into Oneonta Creek. And shortly after I took this shot, trees fell into the stream, created miniature dams, and obstructed the water flow near this spot. The area was closed indefinitely due to the hazard, so I couldn't take this shot today. Fortunately, because this earth-shattering event occurred at night, nobody was injured in this popular spot.

42-CATHEDRAL PEAK, COLUMBIA RIVER HIGHWAY-OREGON.

Except for the height of the trees along the side of the road, this area has changed little over the last century.

Oneonta Tunnel, circa 1915–1918

This image dramatizes the changes along Oregon's highways. As you can see, the tunnel is now backfilled, the main highway is where the train tracks used to be, and the train tracks are now to the north of the highway.

While I was photographing this spot, a busload of local high school students arrived, ready to photograph and explore the gorge. I showed them Gifford's working print, then let them check the view through my 4x5" camera. As you'd expect, each student had a differing opinion on where I should move my camera.

Bonneville, *Fish Hatchery,* after 1910

"I never saw a finer fish hatchery than the Oregon State Hatchery at Bonneville," said Edwin Sweet, a Commerce Department official, after touring the facility in 1916. The Central Hatchery near Bonneville was considered a national model. Sweet explained that federal appropriations had to spread among a number of plants. Oregon, however, devoted all its hatchery budget to this one.

Central Salmon Hatchery of the State of Oregon, May 1999

Since the Gifford image was labeled "Central Salmon Hatchery," I first thought the location was in central Oregon. Fortunately, I noticed Aldrich Butte in the photograph, which led us to the renamed Bonneville Hatchery. After walking the grounds, we spotted Gifford's location near the offices and decided to explain our project to the employees so as not to alarm them. When we showed the Gifford print to a hatchery employee, he was intrigued. They had the same print — along with others — in their offices, but their copies had no signatures, so they hadn't known the history.

Columbia River Highway, *Eagle Creek Bridge,* after 1915

Gifford captured this image of Eagle Creek Bridge's east end shortly after its completion in November 1915. The approaches to the viaduct follow the natural terrain, and highway designer Samuel Lancaster was particularly proud of the stonework on the bridge. From I-84, you can spot this bridge, which is used today to access the parking lot of Punchbowl Falls.

Because I've been across this bridge more times than I care to remember, I was looking forward to discovering the changes that have taken place over the years. While setting up to photograph the Eagle Creek parking lot exit bridge (east abutment), I compared the view with the vintage Gifford print. Part of the elegant railings, with the arched openings, are gone, and the two-way bridge is now a one-way road. While I was photographing this scene, my son and his dog Stihl stood on the bridge, watching the salmon migrate upstream as my father and I used to do years ago.

Columnbia River Highway, *Eagle Creek Bridge,* after 1915

May 1999

I wanted to reshoot the Eagle Creek Bridge when the water was low, so we returned in late spring/early summer. This time, we found a small gravel bed near Gifford's original location. Backwater from Bonneville Dam, which was built thirty years after Gifford took his photograph, has raised the water line substantially.

Columbia Gorge, after 1917

While shooting Columbia Gorge looking east from Women's Forum Park, we had an interesting chance encounter with a couple that was passing by. Intrigued by our truck and camera, they struck up a conversation with us. My son launched into his almost memorized speech about the book project and handed over the Gifford print for them to inspect. Within seconds, the gentleman asked if this was the Benjamin Gifford of yesteryear and if he had a son named Ralph. When I said yes, he said he worked with Ralph at the Oregon State Highway Department for years, proving that it really is a small world.

Columbia Gorge, after 1917

One of the most photographed panoramic vistas in the Northwest, this view graced some of Gifford's top-selling postcards. It encompasses the Columbia River Gorge, Crown Point, Vista House, Rooster Rock, and Beacon Rock. With alterations to the landscape such as the opening of the Columbia River Highway and construction of the Vista House atop Crown Point, photographers frequently updated their postcard shots of this scene. Although Gifford had been photographing this point for almost twenty years, the rapid development of the highway around 1915 rendered his current photos as historic with each new season.

Crown Point Vista House, after 1917

Constructed in 1917, this building was dedicated on May 5, 1918. Originally, the décor included giant enlargements of Gifford's best Columbia River photographs, some of which were printed on glass and illuminated from behind by daylight. According to local historians, these prints graced the building until World War II, when they were taken down in fear that the Vista House might be bombed. In addition, rumor had it that a spy was in the area, so the remaining Gifford prints and other fixtures were removed for safekeeping — never to be replaced. The original glass enlargements made a brief reappearance at a country auction held around 1960, but today most are lost.

Hood River, *Oak Street,* before 1911

In this shot, you'll notice the streetlight is electric and the plank sidewalk on the right is being replaced with concrete.

Hood River, *Hotel Oregon,* circa 1909

The main building of this historic hotel was constructed at 2nd Street and Cascade Avenue in 1903. An enlargement project in 1909 added a four-story annex (at left) and a trellised rooftop garden to the roof of the original building. Gifford took this shot shortly after the additions were complete. In 1911, the charming veranda, offering views stretching to the Columbia River, was permanently removed when the plank sidewalk was replaced with concrete. The hotel, later renamed the Waucoma Hotel, also served as the Chamber of Commerce and a Greyhound bus station. The fire marshal closed the building in 1973. The hotel is now listed on the National Register of Historic Places, but remains mostly vacant.

Waucoma Hotel Building, May 1999

I'd passed this building, located along one of the main roads through Hood River, many times. But I never would have recognized it from the Gifford print. Tom Robinson tried to prepare us with prints from the 1950s, but even that didn't foreshadow the real experience. The building was a shell of its former glory, and curious passersby were astounded by the Gifford print we showed them. We hope this comparison encourages an investor to restore this hotel to its former striking self.

Hood River, *First National Bank,* 1910

In this 1910 photograph, the First National Bank building is finished and open for business, but the buildings on either side are still under construction.

Finding this bank turned out to be a wild goose chase. An old Gifford print indicated the bank was in The Dalles, so we spent the good part of a morning checking out every building in the city. Finally, we decided to give up and consult Tom. Heading back from a trip to eastern Oregon, Tom duplicated our fruitless search for the bank in The Dalles. After giving up, he continued homeward, stopping in Hood River for lunch. From his seat in the restaurant, he spotted the building.

Hood River, circa 1915–1917

When I visited this spot one morning, I decided that it would photograph best in the afternoon, so I planned to return later in the day. On my first visit, a fisherman heading down to the river to try his luck greeted me. Coincidentally, on my return visit a few hours later, the man once again greeted me, this time on his way back from the river. He informed me that he had caught no fish and suggested that I try my hand at fishing, considering my patience to wait all day to take a photo.

Columbia River Tunnel on the Oregon River & Navigation Railroad, circa 1901

Union Pacific Tunnel, April 1999

Gifford copyrighted this early view of the Oregon River & Navigation Railroad (later Union Pacific) in 1901. The train tunnel, located two miles east of Hood River, is visible from eastbound I-84.

At first, the dramatic changes in the rock formations in this area made me think I was in the wrong spot. But I soon learned that, years ago, road construction crews blew the north side of the formations to smithereens to make way for the I-84 freeway. To reproduce the vintage print, I had to stand on live railroad tracks on a blind corner. We calculated that I had four seconds from the time we would first see an engine until it would roll over my camera position. Not wanting to become part of history myself, I waited for the next train to pass, then hurried out to see how lucky I'd be that day.

In Gifford's description of this photograph of Pulpit Rock, he said, "Joseph Luxillo, an Indian who was baptized at the Methodist Mission in about 1840, remembers the early missionaries preaching to the Indians from the top of this rock, on which Daniel Lee chiseled out a seat and called the Indians from a great distance, by blowing a long tin horn." Taken near the present East 12th and Court Streets, Gifford's shot shows Luxillo (alternately spelled Luxello) demonstrating Lee's position on the basaltic pillar.

"What a peculiar place for a monolith," I thought, the first time I laid eyes on this area in the 1970s. I wasn't aware of the landmark's history as a preaching spot until I revisited it in the early 1990s while photographing historic places along the Oregon Trail. So even though I'd been to Pulpit Rock, when Tom showed me the Gifford print, I couldn't believe it. Pulpit Rock stood proudly, like a stone warrior, above the Columbia River. One of my favorite retakes, this image shows the rock now surrounded by concrete and homes. Today people seldom take the time to glance at this historic pillar, buzzing by it in autos and trucks as if it were a bother.

The Dalles, *Columbia River Looking Southwest,* circa 1900

In 1900 Gifford copyrighted this photograph, one of his many images of The Dalles. The blotched sky is a result of damage to Gifford's original negative over the years.

A few weeks after this retake, a fire burned the grain elevators (near the freeway) to the ground. So now both of our images are historic.

Mill Creek Valley, *South of The Dalles,* circa 1910

September 1999

The Dalles Business Men's Association published this photograph in a booster pamphlet called "The Dalles and Dufur." The original caption described the scene as "General Orchard view in Mill Creek Valley, showing how the land appeared prior to clearing, and the results that have been attained."

With all the orchards now dotting the valley, we had a difficult time finding Gifford's original location. On the right behind the fruit trees, you'll see the two buildings from the original photograph.

Fifteenmile Creek and Covington Point, circa 1906

December 1999

Published in the 1906 pamphlet "Some Views of The Dalles, Oregon and Vicinity," this image features two cow barns, a foot bridge, a railroad bridge, a cookhouse, railroad siding to Seufert cannery, a cannery office, Seufert's cannery, and the Columbia River.

This same view of The Dalles now shows Fifteenmile Creek, the Seufert Viaduct, the I-84 freeway, and Fifteenmile Road. You can see more of The Dalles and Mt. Hood in the background.

Celilo Falls, circa 1897–1912

Gifford shot this image of the Columbia River looking northeast from Seufert's Tumwater Fishwheel No. 1 before the construction of the Celilo Canal. Celilo Falls, known in Gifford's day as Tumwater Falls, was located eleven miles east of The Dalles on the Columbia, and the image includes Big Island, Horseshoe Falls, Chiefs Islands, and Taffe Fishwheels.

This view of the Columbia River, shot from the railroad track embankment, now overlooks the Wishram Railroad Village on the Washington side. Backwaters of The Dalles Dam, approximately ten miles downstream, permanently submerged Celilo Falls in 1957.

Mt. Hood from Lost Lake, 1899

One of Gifford's most famous early photographs, "Sunrise on Mt. Hood from Lost Lake," is the result of numerous attempts to capture this spot. A newspaper article published shortly after the picture was taken related that this photograph of "Mt. Hood and the lake had been taken at sunrise. It shows the reflection of the mountain in the lake as plainly as it shows the mountain itself. One end of the lake is as calm as can be while a beautiful ripple plays on the other end. Good judges pronounce this one of the handsomest pictures of the mountain and the lake ever made." The newspaper then quoted Gifford directly: "'Everything was just right when we got in there,' said Mr. Gifford. 'We went in one day and out the next, making three negatives while there. I doubt if I could get such another exposure in a year as this one was.'" Gifford frequently advertised that he was offered $1,000 for the original negative but refused it.

November 1999

Mt. Hood from Sandy River, after 1908

November 1999

In this classic Then & Now shot, the changes in the image speak for themselves.

Mt. Hood from Summit Prairie, circa 1897–1918

The postcard of this image, which Gifford produced late in his career, is signed "Gifford Scenic Photos."

Mt. Hood from Summit Meadows, July 1999

Over time, the prairie was dubbed a meadow. Although I'd been to this area many times, I never knew there was a building and corral in the meadow at one time. I did know, however, that a small historic pioneer cemetery was located on the edge of this mountain prairie.

Arrah Wanna Inn, after 1918

Early advertising boasted "Whatever Your Bent — you will like Arrah Wanna." Shortly after the lodge purchased a radio with a loudspeaker, its brochure bragged about dancing: "With furniture back and rugs rolled up, a maple floor, spacious and splendid, is at your disposal." At roaring '20s prices, a couple could stay the night and have breakfast the next morning for $8.75. Although Gifford's postcard says the Inn is in Brightwood, it is actually closer to Wemme.

Arrah Wanna Lodge, July 1999

A local real estate agent helped us find this property, forty-three miles from Portland at Salmon River. The lodge is now a private religious camp for young adults, and the management graciously allowed us to shoot from the property.

Gifford's White River Studio, after 1918

WHITE RIVER STUDIO, MT. HOOD LOOP ROAD - OREGON.

Benjamin Gifford's son Ralph operated this photo studio and postcard stand after his World War I naval discharge until about 1928. Ralph went on to create the photo department of the Oregon State Highway Commission, and R.M. Filloon, a photographer from The Dalles, took over the studio. Eventually, a flood of the White River washed out the structure.

Old US 30 at White River Bridge, August 1999

The site of Gifford's old studio is now across the highway from a Boy Scout camp.

Deschutes River, circa 1897–1918

Recently, biologists and fish and wildlife experts rediscovered one of these Gifford photographs of the Deschutes riverbanks. To analyze the impact of railroad tracks installed along the course of the river, researchers use Gifford's early photographs of vegetation growth.

January 2000

Gifford made dozens of images of the Deschutes River, some of which were identified and some of which were not. Although one of these Gifford images was unidentified, vegetation in the region indicated that it was the Columbia River Gorge. Still, I needed some type of landmark for precise identification. While studying the images, I noticed a small railroad trestle on the other side of the river. I'd visited the exact spot in pursuit of my other hobby— rock collecting.

Sherar's Bridge, *Deschutes River,* circa 1897–1918

December 1999

Sherar's Bridge, a forty-foot-wide narrows on the Deschutes River, was the first of many bridges built here since 1862. The channel is bound by tall rock walls on either side, and is the best natural bridge location in the entire canyon. When the area's post office opened in 1862, the community was named Deschutes. The bridge served as a gateway to the gold mines in Central Oregon. When Joe Sherar bought the bridge in 1871, he invested his fortune in improving the roads leading to it. In 1883, Sherar renamed the location after himself. State Highway 216 now crosses the Deschutes River at this location and a thirty-room hotel dating from the stage-stop days is long gone.

Sherar's Bridge, *Deschutes River,* circa 1897–1918

August 1999

Smith Rocks, *Crooked River,* circa 1897–1918

This two-part panorama of Smith Rocks shows Three Sisters in the background. One recent study commissioned by Portland General Electric used these Gifford photographs as a point of comparison in evaluating riparian vegetation. The study suggests that grazing may have reduced the vegetation when Gifford photographed the scene.

August 1999

Our view of Smith Rocks includes Crooked River and Mt. Jefferson. Despite the narrowing of the river channel, many more juniper trees exist in the area today. Smith Rocks has survived recent attempts at development and also receives more environmental protection today. To take this photograph, we left home at 3:00 a.m. in hopes of capturing the location in the early morning light. Unfortunately, when we arrived, clouds blocked the sun. To kill time until the sun rose above the bank of clouds, I decided to take a short walk. When I got back a short time later, I found on my truck a ticket for illegal camping! With my son sawing logs in the front seat, it sure looked that way. I found the park manager, explained my situation, and we settled out of court.

Fossil, circa 1897–1918

October 1999

In less than twenty-five years, Fossil evolved dramatically from its commercial genesis, a claim shack that sold tobacco and overalls in 1877. The second enterprise, a liquor and drug store, qualified Fossil as a stage stop. This led to a restaurant, hotel, and other businesses, and soon the town needed a newspaper to keep up with the frontier politics and economics. In a hotly contested move, area residents carved their own 54- by 30-mile county out of Giliam County in 1899. The new county was named Wheeler, and Fossil became the county seat. By 1902, the town had waterworks and an electric plant. The population leveled around 1910, staying at about 500 for the next forty years.

To capture this view of Fossil from above, we had to hike a steep hill on a hot fall day. Bad timing! Part of the way up, I sat on a rock to rest, but jumped up as soon as I touched the stone. Something had bit the back of my knee. As I viewed the two small, red, swollen puncture marks, my first thought was rattlesnake. My son searched around for the culprit, but found nothing. Fortunately, I could still walk, so we continued up the hill. To this day, we have no clue what bit me.

Fossil, circa 1897–1918

October 1999

I was photographing this image of Fossil from below, with my head under the dark cloth, when I felt a strong nudge. I admonished my son to quit messing around — I was in a hurry because the light was fading. No response. I heard a strange sound and poked my head out to see what was going on. To my surprise, about a half dozen horses were gathered behind me, probably thinking I was either food or a new salt lick. My son, who had walked back to the truck to retrieve my film, watched the whole episode unfold from a distance. All I could hear coming from the truck was his loud laughter. The shadow in the bottom right corner offers proof of the strange encounter: the ghostly form is me under the dark cloth, and to my right is the curious horse!

Ashwood, *Trout Creek and Ash Butte,* circa 1897–1918

Gifford usually visited this town with his traveling tent studio during his spring tours; the 1904 Ashwood Prospector *even advertised which week he would be there. At the beginning of the twentieth century, the* Ashwood Prospector *summarized the advantages of the community, noting the "location of the town is all that could be desired, being in the very heart of the mining district and on a beautiful level valley with the cool mountain stream, Trout Creek, flowing through." The editorial continued, "Ashwood is just the place that is destined to become one of the leading towns of Eastern Oregon and in a few years will be seen, instead of a score of houses and a few hundred people, a city of substantial buildings, diversified enterprises and thousands of people."*

Today, the community in the valley is probably more attractive than Ashwood's bygone boosters predicted.

Benham Rapids, *Deschutes River,* circa 1897–1918

Gifford considered Benham Rapids, located on the Deschutes River, among his favorite subjects. Near this scene, two competing railroads raced construction crews up each side of the river, laying track in a contest to dominate regional transportation.

Boulevard from The Dalles to Mill Creek Valley, circa 1910

This photograph was published in "The Dalles and Dufur Oregon" booster pamphlet around 1910; the caption described it as "Boulevard leading from The Dalles to Mill Creek valley. Orchards and vineyards in the background with Mt. Hood in the distance."

Dufur, circa 1909

When Gifford photographed this city in 1909, stores lined both sides of the main street. As in many central Oregon communities, fruit trees bloomed in Dufur for a while but the ground wasn't moist enough to sustain them. The town hosted the largest fruit farm in the world, but by the 1920s the farm replaced its orchards with wheat. Today, irrigation has brought back the orchards, and the town is a well-preserved example of an early 1900s community. We highly recommend the town rummage sale that Dufur hosts every spring.

Setting up a camera near the middle of the street in a small town is bound to attract attention. Four people, who happened to be members of the town's historical society, traipsed out of a nearby building to ask what we were photographing. When we explained the Then & Now project, they were quite excited by the inclusion of Dufur. Then, when I mentioned we were from Portland, they asked if we knew a photographer named Steve Terrill. They had one of my images of a historical home in Portland called the Zimmerman House and were actually related to the Zimmerman family. I introduced myself and we all marveled at the chances of meeting like this in a small central Oregon town.

White River Falls Electric Plant, circa 1910

Located twenty-seven miles south of The Dalles, the White River Falls electric plant was built in the fall of 1901 to supply the nearby town with power for its first electric streetlights. Gifford's image probably shows the plant's reconstruction in the late summer of 1910.

In the last month of the twentieth century, amidst nationwide concerns about terrorism overtaking millennium celebrations, the local media were covering the possibility of bombers targeting electrical towers in the Wild West. When we hiked out to this spot, we wondered if Big Brother was watching our every move. Carrying tripods and cases, we probably did look a little suspicious. The park was closed when we took this shot and we never saw a soul save the sparse vehicles that drove by on the main road and echoed through the hills. Although nobody approached us, a state police officer did pass by slowly — but maybe it was just a coincidence.

Three Sisters, circa 1897–1918

Gifford's view of the Three Sisters is from the west.

After searching down every back road near the small town of Sisters, we finally located Gifford's original spot. We hiked through the private property, only to encounter numerous trees blocking our view. When we relocated a little farther east, we discovered a farmer's field with bales of hay that emulated the stones Gifford used in his image. In hopes of duplicating the vintage print, I set up my 4x5" camera and instructed my son to strike a pose.

Drake's Sawmill on the Deschutes River, *Bend,* circa 1907

This photograph shows Drake's original sawmill on the Deschutes River, between the Farewell Bend Ranch and Sisemore's Bridge.

Columbia Park and the Deschutes River, August 1999

The trail that this photograph was taken from seemed like a safe place to set up my camera. But I had barely finished when a high-speed bicyclist clipped the tripod, nearly sending my camera into the Deschutes River for an unscheduled cleaning. I had to call upon my son's intimidating presence to keep the peace on the riverside trail.

Bend, *Drake Home,* circa 1901–1910

Built in 1901 by Bend's founder, A.M. Drake, this beautiful hunting lodge was decorated with Oriental rugs and Chinese lanterns. The lodge stood where Drake Park is now, next to Mirror Pond on the Deschutes River. When the Drakes moved out in 1912, the cabin became home for Bend's Emblem Club, a commercial club sponsoring booster events to promote the fast-growing community. In ten short years, Bend rose from practically nothing to a complete city. The lodge was torn down in 1956, but the site is marked with a plaque.

Drake Park, August 1999

Not a single person could help us find the location for Gifford's original, unidentified image. On a trip to central Oregon, we decided to capture some images in Bend, including the area around Mirror Pond. While checking out the area, I walked over to the Rademacher House. To my surprise, I found an information sign at the base of a ponderosa pine bearing the exact same photograph of the print I was holding.

Bend, Bond Street, 1916

This photograph shows the new O'Kane building, on the corner of Oregon Street. It replaced the Hotel Oregon, which burned down the previous year. Between 1910 and 1920, the population of Bend exploded from 536 to 5,414.

This image of Bend from the corner of Greenwood proves that persistence is rewarded. After driving hundreds of miles to take this picture, we were continually dissatisfied with the results. The problem of shooting in just the right light — without traffic interference — is familiar to photographers. And photographers who shoot in black & white will immediately understand the problem with trying to capture a range of light far beyond what a film can record on their negative. We reconsidered our methods and decided to postpone further efforts until fall, when the trees explode in color — and we were rewarded with this color image.

In this image of Bend from the late summer of 1910, you'll see the Deschutes River in the foreground; the Bend Water, Light, and Power Dam in the center; and Newport Street (during its final stages of construction) at the right. The backwater from the dam forms Mirror Pond Lake. At the left, you can see the initial work on the powerhouse; after its completion, generators were installed, and Bend's electric service was inaugurated November 9, 1910.

August 1999

Matlock Ranch, circa 1897–1918

Morrow County will not soon forget the Matlock brothers. The duo virtually saved the populations of Lexington and Ione during the 1903 flood that wiped out Heppner. A huge tidal wave, born of a cloudburst, rolled down the canyon and crashed into Heppner, ripping buildings right out of the dirt and killing more than 300 people. Within seconds, the flood became Oregon's deadliest disaster of the twentieth century. When the Matlocks witnessed the flood, they jumped on their horses and raced ahead of the surging floodwaters to yell warnings in every direction, saving countless lives with their breakneck ride.

Morrow County, October 1999

Although people in Heppner said the Matlock Ranch was five or ten miles east of town, we spent almost a whole day driving around Morrow County looking for it. We were hoping to get this shot in one day, but as fate would have it, the sun set less than fifteen minutes before our arrival. We missed the shot and had to return the next day. After all, when a photographer captures a scene, he or she is not photographing the subject but, rather, photographing the light the scene reflects. Though this point may seem arcane, it's more than semantic — the light tells the whole story of what goes on the film and how it looks. What appears at first glance to be a no-problem shot can easily take your schedule book and file it under fiction.

Umatilla County, *Elephant Rock,* before 1909

Elephant Rock sits on the old road from Pendleton to Bingham Springs on the Umatilla Indian Reservation. In the early 1900s, stagecoach drivers often made an unscheduled stop here on the way to the springs to accommodate Pendleton's many Kodakers (tourists). The landmark sits high on a ridge overlooking the Umatilla River.

October 1999

Having never seen or heard of Elephant Rock — and impressed by Gifford's image — I was anxious to discover this location. I called the visitor's center in Pendleton, and they assured me that Elephant Rock was still there and provided directions. On the day of this shoot, we headed up a gravel road in search of a small sign indicating the trailhead. Unfortunately, the deteriorated, bullet-ridden sign was hidden in overgrown bushes, and we drove miles too far before finally locating the rock formation.

On November 1, 1915, W. Farra and Indian Agent Charles S. Heinline visited Chief Captain Louie (ca. 1845–1935) and the Paiute Indian camp, near the present site of the Old Camp Casino. According to the Burns Times-Herald, *Heinline distributed twenty-four wool blankets and fourteen army surplus tents to the tribe that day. The Paiutes used the tents through 1928.*

In 1928, housing replaced the army surplus tents; in the early 1930s, the Paiute Reservation was moved to the other side of Burns.

Crater Lake Lodge, June 30, 1914

November 1999

Since the lodge was under construction in Gifford's image, we had trouble pinpointing his location. The lodge had been expanded over the years, but the chimney stayed in place and helped us decide on our final location.

Crater Lake, circa 1914

November 1999

Gifford's photographs of this area show cars parked in the foreground, so I thought I'd sneak my truck up the access road to the rim for the shot — but I got busted. In desperation, I carried my camera up to the viewpoint to take the shot, cars or not. At the mountaintop, a mighty gust of wind tore my faxes of the working prints out of my grasp and blew them down the caldera. After climbing down to retrieve them and hiking back up, I was cold and wet. The soggy faxes seemed unsure whether to freeze into sheets of ice or simply disintegrate into paper fiber. With the wind blowing so strongly that I had to hold the tripod down and my hands so cold they froze to the aluminum, I still managed to load the sheet film holders into the camera and make the exposures. I'm just glad the pictures turned out beautifully, and they will always remind me of the wonderful nature walks I had while photographing them!

Crater Lake, circa 1914

November 1999

The known history of Oregon's only national park, Crater Lake, has been intertwined with photographer-explorers. Historians long believed that Peter Britt, Jacksonville, Oregon's pioneer daguerreotypist, produced the first photographs of Crater Lake in 1874. His widely published images put Crater Lake on the map and, in 1902, helped persuade Congress to pass the act that created the park. Later research indicated that the Sutton expedition took the first photographs in 1869. In 1885, explorer and amateur photographer Will Steele named Wizard Island, which towers 753 feet above the lake. These early explorers endured extreme hardships to make their images, and the danger of the work became tragically apparent in 1913 when noted photographer B. B. Bakowski died of exposure while working at Crater Lake.

Medford, *City Park,* 1905–1909

At the height of the town's orchard boom, the Medford Commercial Club published a booklet featuring Gifford's photography. This Gifford photograph of Medford City Park, taken sometime after 1905 when the fountain was complete, shows improvements to the park financed by local civic groups and fraternal organizations. One reviewer noted that the booklet was "handsomer than the souvenir booklets ordinarily sold to tourists." (You can see a color reproduction of this booklet's cover on page 13.) The city was swamped with inquiries from easterners, and land sales boomed. However, the ground was unable to sustain the new orchards and many trees died. Within five years, the population dropped by almost a third.

Medford Area, circa 1909

In our search for Gifford's location, we ended up on Foothill Road looking at Coker Butte (at right). Development in the Rogue River Valley presented a problem. Gifford's camera position had probably been leveled years ago and we couldn't proceed farther up the hill due to the electrical power station and surrounding homes. I posed my son in the driver's seat of my 1989 Toyota 4Runner and attempted to re-create Gifford's image.

Gifford published this photograph, "Near Fort Klamath," in his 1909 book Art Works of the State of Oregon.

While scouting near Fort Klamath, we asked nearly everyone we came across about the location of this image. Believe it or not, just about everyone we spoke to thought it was not even located in the valley. With our hopes diminishing at a rapid pace, we headed down every major and secondary road we could find. Finally, we decided to head to the west side of Klamath Lake for a different shot. Toward the end of the open valley the hills started to take on a familiar shape, and there before us was Gifford's shot.

Gold Ray, *Table Rock,* before 1909

Gifford published this image in his 1909 book Art Works of the State of Oregon *as "Gold Ray, Table Rock in the Distance." Local boosters christened the recently constructed Golden Drift Dam "The Niagara of the Pacific Coast" and in 1911 estimated that it "had energy enough for all the traffic and wheels of manufacture in the state."*

Vegetation prospered on this hillside over the decades, so to our dismay this was the absolute highest we could climb before heading into the trees. We explored every possible option for the retake, but never could get a clear opening for a better vantage point.

Gifford published "Klamath Marsh" as a photogravure in his 1909 book Art Works of the State of Oregon.

In search of Gifford's location, we explored the west side of Klamath Lake for most of a day and even got permission to check out private property. We decided to expand our search to the north, and luckily we spotted the buttes on the distant horizon from a small bend in the road.

Lake of the Woods and Mt. McLoughlin, before 1909

November 1999

The Oregonian *reviewed an early Gifford exhibition and claimed that "Mr. Gifford considers this lake, lying in between Ashland and Crater Lake, and a short distance from Pelican Bay, as one of the loveliest spots on earth."*

To view these scenes, we traveled through virtual ghost towns in which the majority of homes were summer getaways. Without a soul in sight, it was eerie. When we walked the shoreline in search of Gifford's location, we ran into a few suspicious people who wanted to know what we were doing. Once we described the project, they figured we were OK. But they did confess to copying down my license plate number earlier in the day in case we were up to no good!

Lake of the Woods and Mt. McLoughlin, before 1909

November 1999

To make this image, my son and I had to race to our destination because the light was fading fast. We parked our truck and sprinted like heck to the water's edge. In our scurry through the trees, a limb caught my shirt and jerked me to the ground. After brushing myself off, I arrived at the scene to find my tripod already set up and my son laughing at what he described as a bear sprinting through the woods and disappearing into a clump of branches — but the bear just happened to be me!

Mt. Washington in Cascade Range, before 1909

Gifford published this image, "Mt. Washington in Cascade Range," as a photogravure in his 1909 book Art Works of the State of Oregon.

Mt. Washington and Big Lake, October 1999

Although I've photographed this area many times, I was amazed when I compared the view with Gifford's print. Much of the lake had seemingly receded, giving way to the encroaching vegetation.

Sutherlin Creek near Roseburg, before 1909

Gifford published this image, "Sutherlin Creek Near Roseburg," as a photogravure in his 1909 book Art Works of the State of Oregon.

April 1999

With only the simple title of "Sutherlin Creek" to work with, we were in for a long, frustrating search. After we had been driving around for hours, my son woke up from a nap and asked if I'd found it yet. I gave him the old print and told him to find it. He glanced out the window, his eyes barely open, and pointed with a seer's sense to the precise location. We were on the main road through Sutherlin and he had recognized the tree-covered slopes between a few homes. Although I assumed the quaint bridge would be long gone, I was expecting a park or scenic area. Over the years, the picturesque creek had been channeled ruler-straight, and developers had constructed an eloquent case for urban renewal.

Grants Pass, *6th and D Streets,* circa 1910

Grants Pass completed the rebuilding of Sixth Street in November 1910 to the tune of $100,000. The project included burying the water pipes, sewer pipes, power lines, and phone wires underground; widening the sidewalks; paving the streets with the city's own steam roller; adding the attractive cluster lights; and purchasing an early street-cleaning machine (shown).

We arrived in Grants Pass one evening and started scouting. We were hoping to find the location and be ready to photograph it in the early daylight, but had no luck. The major buildings in Gifford's image had probably fallen to the wrecking ball, so we had very few clues. We started out fresh in the morning, canvassing the old town section until it was time to stop at a local café for breakfast. At that point, we decided to wait for the Josephine County Historical Society to open and seek professional assistance. Unfortunately, they couldn't identify the location either, but they were reasonably sure it was within the downtown core. During one last look, my son spotted an original building from Gifford's image just a half-block down and across the street from where we'd been sitting in the café's window booth.

HOMING IN ON OREGON

By John Daniel

My first view of Oregon was nothing much. In 1966, I navigated a blue and white Jeep with a bad electrical system up the coast from San Francisco, having left my mother's home in Washington, D.C., two weeks earlier. I hit the Oregon border around 1:00 a.m. on a very foggy night in late summer and pulled into a state campground north of Brookings. I parked the Jeep on a downslope, stumbled toward the beach in the thick dark, sat on a rock, and let the boom and wash and shrill withdrawing hiss of breakers soothe my overheated head. After a while I went down to touch the Pacific. In the morning the Jeep started without a rolling jump, which I took to be a sign.

I was on my way to Reed College in Portland, where I would try to be a student—and would succeed for a year and a half. My relations with my new natural surroundings turned out to be far less problematic than my relations with books and classrooms. At some point in the fall of my freshman year, a shot of lightning exploded the top of one of the tallest trees on campus, a solitary Douglas fir, and turned it into a flaming torch. I wasn't lucky enough to see the strike, but I did come along in time to watch yellow flames blazing a hundred feet overhead in the top of a wet, dark tree. Another sign. "This," I said to myself, "is a cool place."

My enthusiasm waxed further a year later, when a ripping windstorm blew in off the Pacific. On campus with friends, I watched trees snapping and tumbling on the other side of the river in southwest Portland, taking down power lines and popping a transformer now and then with a hail of sparks. We hollered and cheered, far better situated (as I would learn) than Lewis and Clark and their men had been in 1805. Newly arrived at the mouth of the Columbia, mildewed and sleepless from flea bites and living on roots and bad salmon loaf, the explorers were assaulted by a similar December storm. "The winds violent," wrote William Clark in his journal. "Trees falling in every derection, whorl winds, with gusts of rain Hail & Thunder, this kind of weather lasted all day. Certainly one of the worst days that ever was!"

It was Oregon, wild and lovely Oregon, that ruined my academic career. How could I keep my nose in Herodotus and my ears in windy seminars while surrounded by a green paradise of mountains, rivers, seacoast, and forests of gargantuan trees? So I traded Reed

College for a tin hardhat. I dropped out and went to work for a while as a logger, my enthusiasm dissolving any sense of contradiction between loving the trees of paradise and leveling them. I also launched into backpacking and mountain climbing. On Mt. Hood, my first big climb, I couldn't believe my eastern eyes. I was standing 11,000 feet in the air atop a snowbound volcano with nothing around me but everything, an oceanic vista such as I had never imagined, the wavy verdant landscape with its roads and towns and other human marks—trifles by eastern standards, mere chicken scratches—stretching vastly in every direction, the Cascades punctuated with snowy volcanic exclamations: St. Helens (still a perfect cone), Adams, and Rainier to the north; Jefferson, Jack, Washington, and the Three Sisters to the south.

I left the state several times to pursue my personal confusions in San Francisco, which seemed a necessary thing to do in the late 1960s and early '70s, but I kept coming back. I was in love but didn't quite know it. In 1973, I left the Bay Area for a railroad job in a part of Oregon I hadn't seen, the Klamath Basin, just east of the Cascades and north of the California line. Again I couldn't believe my eyes. Where was the forest? Where were the merry streams, the emerald meadows? Seven years after first setting foot in the state, it was just dawning on me that two-thirds of Oregon is dry plateau. "Won't stay long here," I said to myself.

I stayed ten years. Bleakness turned to beauty before my eyes. My spirit opened in the bright spacious distances of rimrocks and alkali lakes and junipered hills, of mountains blue on the horizon, of parklike forests of orange-barked pines and huddled aspens. I gradually discovered the lofty pronghorn pastures of Hart Mountain, the Malheur Refuge with its seasonal bonanzas of birds, the singular standing wave of rock that is Steens Mountain, the ups and downs and tilted vistas of the John Day country, the psychedelic geology of Leslie Gulch, and, far to the northeast, the exuberant granitic Wallowas, nothing like the Cascades, a branch of the Rocky Mountains that got lost and wandered into our state.

Nature, I realized over the years, has a lot on her mind in this state of Oregon, a slew of wildly various thoughts, and she's committed to all of them. Forget the interior, consider the corners alone. The steep slopes of the Klamath Mountains in the southwest host one of the most diverse temperate forests in the world, a hodgepodge of broadleafs and needle trees and a zillion understory species. There are spots on the coast down there, where I first blundered into the state, where palm trees grow. Shoot 400 miles east, to the Owyhee Uplands we share with Idaho and Nevada, and you can walk the lonesome sagebrush tableland all day long without sighting a single trunk, but for a willow or cottonwood in the wanderingly beautiful canyons etched into the land. The Owyhees might get eight inches of moisture a year. Zag to the Clatsop Plain in the northwest corner, where Lewis and Clark and their Corps of Discovery spent their triumphant and miserable winter of 1805–1806, and you'll get 120 inches, up to 200 in the ferned and mossy Coast Range not far south. From that country of rainforest, of storm surf hammering the capes and headlands, vault due eastward to still a different kind of grandeur at a place called Hat Point, beyond the Wallowas, where you'll gaze down almost 6,000 feet into a vast, terraced, grassy-benched vessel of quiet called Hells Canyon. Tiny within its inner chasm, the green Snake River hurls itself through Rush Creek Rapids, its thunderous roil refined at your vantage to soundlessness, a rumor, a whisper of wind.

Of all the states, only California can credibly claim greater variety of landscape and extremes of climate—and California cheats by being so big. I was lured into its bosom again in the 1980s, following the siren song of a writing career, but when I came north again, I came to stay. First in Portland, that good gray city of bridges and bookstores and the best beer in the world, and now on an acre of land tucked up in the Coast Range foothills at the southern end of the Willamette Valley, the New Eden that enticed caravans of settlers over the Oregon Trail in the 1840s and '50s. It's not really much of an Eden. Rains too much. Crawls with slugs and newts and tree frogs. Fungi erupt from the dank soil. Our yard is more moss than grass. My wife and I trudge about in rubber boots, leaving footprints six inches deep. The days are gray and gray and gray. The trees drip. The downspouts gurgle. Then the sun goofs up one day and shows itself. We stagger, dazzled, groping for dark glasses and eyedrops. We listen for the song sparrow, the prophetic honking of geese. A goldfinch flashes. The dogwoods spread a white rumor. Visions appear in the rhododendrons. The green world sparkles.

Eden? All the Eden we need.

❖ ❖ ❖ ❖ ❖

AS THE PHOTOGRAPHS IN THIS BOOK DEMONSTRATE, things change around here. And as they also demonstrate, things stay pretty much the same, especially the things of nature we touch lightly or not at all. I find it reassuring that the land abides, little impressed with our human doings. But in the vastness of its own time it changes ceaselessly. This land *is* change.

The bedrock of our state is a cobbled-together raft of several island masses carried eastward by tectonic movement to fuse one against another over the course of a hundred million years or so. The Cascades rose and continue to create themselves out of the volcanic violence engendered by one crustal plate slipping stubbornly beneath another. Only seventeen million years ago — yesterday, geologically speaking — the stretched and faulted skin of what is now high desert gave forth colossal sheets of lava that spread hundreds of miles, clear to the coast, and hardened one atop another into a bed of basalt up to two miles thick. In the last two million years, successive waves of groaning ice covered and carved the Wallowas and the Elkhorns, Steens Mountain and the Strawberry Range, Gearhart Mountain and the High Cascades. As the ice withdrew,

streams and rivers flowed in its great tracks; shrubs and grasses and forests slowly resurrected themselves.

Even the most recent split second of geologic time, the last 15,000 years, has been lively with change — all too lively, I bet, for the Native Americans who may have been here that long or longer. A series of the greatest floods in the planet's known history swept

> *Photography extends and clarifies our view.
> We see what we have built or broken,
> what we have saved or forfeited, what we have left
> alone, or taken, or taken and relinquished.
> We see, for better or for worse, what we have done.*

boulders bound in floes of ice from a collapsing glacial lake in Montana to resting places throughout our placid Willamette Valley, periodically drowning the present site of Portland under 400 feet of muddy water. After the floods, fire. Seven millenniums ago, a mountain we never knew, probably bigger than any now present in the Oregon Cascades, blew off six cubic miles of magma before collapsing, cooling, and gradually filling with what would become the pellucid blue waters of Crater Lake. As the Pleistocene climate warmed and dried, broader and shallower lakes to the east evaporated, forests receded up mountain slopes, and mastodon and three-toed horse and a species of beaver seven feet long slipped out of the landscape into extinction.

By geologic standards, human beings have done nothing of consequence to the Oregon land. Not the Native Americans, hunting and fishing and foraging through countless seasons, continually setting fire to grasslands and woodlands to condition them for game and edible plants. Not Lewis and Clark, not Peter Skene Ogden or Donald McKenzie, not the North West Company or Hudson's Bay trappers, not the Methodist or Catholic missionaries, not the midwestern immigrants who broke the Willamette Valley sod, not the eager gold grubbers of the Rogue River country and the northeast corner, not the industrial fishermen who mined the prodigal Snake and Columbia salmon runs, not the eastern Oregon stockmen or farmers, not the canneries or the pulp mills, not the loggers or the

merchants or the engineers. Railroads, highways, dams, clearcuts, the Wells Fargo Tower, even our unique state capitol building in Salem, designed to resemble a bowling trophy — nothing at all, the merest ephemera, flicks of a chickadee's wings. (Which is why few geologists are environmental activists. Their sense of time prevents them from getting exercised, though they in turn are viewed by cosmologists as overly fussy and obsessed with minutiae.)

So why do we care? Why do we examine these pairs of pictures with such an alert interest, remarking on the differences and similarities? Why does it give us a spooky pleasure to study images twinned, but not identically? Why does it shock us to see ostensible twins that scarcely look related? Because we are not rocks or rivers or Douglas firs. Because we are sentient and transient and small, but large to our own selves in the tiny nick of time we inhabit. Because we place ourselves, define our sense of home, by the look of the land and the marks we make on it. We don't live long enough to see much of the movement of the greater story, the story of stars, planets, volcanism, rainfall, rivers, the greening of the world with life. But we do see the human story in our places of living, the story we have coauthored with past generations and the places themselves. Photography extends and clarifies our view. We see what we have built or broken, what we have saved or forfeited, what we have left alone, or taken, or taken and relinquished. We see, for better or for worse, what we have done.

❖ ❖ ❖ ❖ ❖

THE HOUSE MY WIFE AND I SHARE, usually with a freeloading pack rat, stands in a grove of adolescent and mature Douglas firs that keeps us cool in summer and keeps us alert, hoping for the endurance of roots and fiber, when the wind comes up in the winter. The view beyond our trees is limited to our farmer neighbor's woods to the west and south, and our rancher neighbor's pasture to the east. This makes us a bit more claustrophobic than most in a naturally claustrophobic climate, and it makes roof-raking a regular chore, but on balance we're glad to live in the enclosure of our grove. You don't necessarily want a distant view in this part of the state, because you can't be sure the modest wooded hills around you are going to look the same next year, next month, or even next week.

You're driving a familiar road within five miles of home, a road you know so well you could steer it in your sleep, and around a curve, could be any curve, there's a vacancy. Light and openness where trees should be. A patch of forest—an acre, ten acres, twenty —*gone*, like Birnam Wood to Dunsinane. Left is a ground-level strew of boughs still vibrant green, splintered limbs, rotten or fractured pieces of trunk, gouts of scraped-up soil, and lots of salal and sword fern that would be blinking, if they had eyes, at the torrent of light. Usually a sparse few trees still stand, scrawny Douglas firs—silly looking without their peer group—or scraggly white oaks or golden chinquapins, maybe a big Doug fir snag or two long past commercial value. And hanging in the air, thick, the sweet fragrance of sap.

If not for our home grove, we would see a fresh clearcut to the south, several old ones to the north, and the potential for many more. The farther hills, the ones we see while driving, sport on their flanks and skylines erratic buzz-cuts weirder than anything kids wear to the mall. I sometimes go walking through a nearby second-growth woods and up a logging road through recent clearcuts, replanted with perky foot-high seedlings, on up to the top of the ridge and then east on the bare ridgetop to a patch of standing timber, left like a topknot on a mostly shaven head. The trees aren't big, which probably explains why they're still upright, except for one— one mossy veteran with a few candelabra limbs the size of modest trees themselves, the whole array rising into a dense crown that somewhere has a top, maybe 150 feet up. The veteran wasn't always alone. Walking the ridgetop—the crest, not where the biggest trees grow—I pass several stumps of ghost trees on the same scale, four and five and six feet in diameter.

The losses are easy to see. A kid walking that ridge in Benjamin Gifford's time saw a forest very different from the partial forest, the reduced forest, the managed forest, a kid sees today. That child of a hundred years ago carried in her mind and heart a different sense of forest—something greater in scale, wilder, more frightening maybe, more beautiful certainly, and more mysterious. That is a loss. The widespread unloveliness of the scalped hills is a loss. If Gifford and Terrill had each taken one statewide photo from a

satellite, one change above all would overpower our attention— the crude geometry of clearcuts and squiggling networks of logging roads up and down the Cascades, up and down the Coast Range, splotched and spotted through the Ochocos and Blues and Wallowas clear to Hells Canyon. And the losses on the ground are not merely aesthetic. There are earthslides where the stripped and road-cut soil couldn't hold, ravaged habitat, silt on the spawning gravels in streams. Native salmon are struggling in the places they've known as home for two million years.

But the story of the landscape is not only about loss. Like most true stories, it's complicated. Those clearcuts tell also of human livings made, food placed on tables, children raised. They tell of millions of dollars in taxes—and federal payments in lieu of taxes—to support schools and other public programs in rural counties. They tell of many thousands of men performing difficult and frequently dangerous labor with spirit, desire, and considerable skill. They tell of families maintaining themselves in communities and landscapes they love through three or four generations by means of work in the woods and mills. They tell of local economies that once thrived, though many are not thriving now. And— a part of the story that should be of keen interest to those who benefit from it—the clearcuts tell of the work's product: the materials that house and shelter and comfort a nation.

> *On my deck I sit squarely involved in that shifting field of human need and desire and awareness and blindness that has shaped the face of Oregon for the cameras of Benjamin Gifford and Steve Terrill, and is shaping it now for the photographers of tomorrow.*

In warm weather I like to sip bourbon in the evening on my back deck, looking south into my neighbor's trees, a stand of tall and stately Douglas firs beginning to develop the mossy, open-park look of the old-growth condition. Sundown turns the green of boughs and moss intensely radiant, a green-gold stillness laced with the songs of finch and sparrow and Swainson's thrush. I enjoy this presence,

never failing to feel lucky, on a deck my stepson constructed of Douglas fir posts and 2x6 lumber. The deck is attached to a house made of beams and studs and joists and rafters, of plywood sheathing and particleboard subfloor, of wood siding and moulding and fascia boards. Within the house are doors and doorframes of wood, furniture of wood, books and magazines and writing pads and other species of paper derived from wood. Within our standing green grove and our neighbor's grove, which spare us the view of clearcuts not far away, we live in a comfortable shell of fallen forest.

I'm glad for the trees I look at and glad for the trees that make up my home. And I'm uneasy, too, until the birds and the bourbon agreeably move my thoughts on, because I know I don't quite get the story. I don't fully accept that I'm in the story, that in a small but significant way I am the story, that my choices or failures to choose are directly related to what I see and don't see around me. I sit where all of us sit, caught up comfortably or not in the dynamic and intricate balance between use and beauty, between self-preservation and preservation of nature, between the demands of economy and the demands of ecology, between the culture of rural localities and the culture of cities and suburbs. On my deck I sit squarely involved in that shifting field of human need and desire and awareness and blindness that has shaped the face of Oregon for the cameras of Benjamin Gifford and Steve Terrill, and is shaping it now for the photographers of tomorrow.

❖ ❖ ❖ ❖ ❖

A FEW YEARS AGO, I was driving through the Klamath Basin, not far from a ranch where I had once lived. It was early March, and the forested peaks—Gearhart, Saddle Mountain, Yainax Butte—still bore the lonely, snowy-blue aspect of winter. The lower country, sage and juniper steppeland patched with pines, was mostly free of snow but still sleeping in its grays, browns, and drab greens. I stopped to walk by the Sycan River, which rises in the meadowy woods north of Gearhart, flows north and west to the Sycan Marsh, and winds south from there through pines and pasture to join the Sprague River near the town of Beatty.

The signatures of the landscape were pleasurably familiar. The roiling tannic current and laughing riffles of the river. Clumps of native bunchgrass among lichened boulders. Lodgepole pines in small stands, the wet duff of their needles fragrant and yielding underfoot, the spent cones crunching. A few tall ponderosas, vibrantly tigerish with their orange, black-furrowed bark, most wildly beautiful of trees—and high in their crowns, singing through numberless boughs of long green needles, the wind's old anthem of solitude and space.

To my eyes and heart, that country is the prettiest in Oregon. In fact, it's the prettiest country I know. I was in no hurry to leave it, so a little later I pulled the truck over at a roadside tavern, a small annex to a general store a few miles east of Chiloquin. The place had a four-stool bar and half a dozen tables. A woman and three men, all in their fifties or sixties, were talking at one of the tables. The woman padded behind the bar in her slippers and served me the beer I ordered.

She and the men resumed their conversation, talking along in the easy manner of friends. Someone had sighted a bear. One of the men was going to grow his tomato plants in a cold frame to protect them from summer frost. This declaration set off a round of ruefully affectionate comments about the climate they shared and endured. "I don't believe we'll get more snow," said one. "Oh, *now* you've done it," shot back another. It was a kind of conversation familiar to me from the years I had lived on the ranch and from my brief stint as a logger. I find it deeply satisfying to hear and make such talk. It's placed talk, laden with smells and colors of the countryside, with knowledge gained from length of living in locality and community.

The woman spoke of a friend who had recently moved up from Los Angeles. "You know what she says about it here, what she loves?" the woman asked, pausing to drag on her cigarette and relish the pleasure of what she was about to report. "She says, 'Up here I've got room to *fluff*!'"

We all laughed. I savored the friend's remark, and the woman's own delight in telling it, as I savored my beer. All of us who live in Oregon, I thought to myself, must feel some version of the same thing. Whether it's physical space we most value, or the informal sociability here, or a less frenetic pace of life, or the freedom to be different, or all of those, we have *room* here, room to shake and

plump our feathers and feel all right. It isn't only a matter of landscape, but the possibility of such freedom begins in landscape—in an uncrowded countryside enjoyed by those who live and make their livings there, and enjoyed as well by visitors who choose to live, or have little choice but to live, in our cities and suburbs. And just as crucially, the possibility of freedom depends on the preservation of wilder landscapes where all human beings are visitors.

When I'd first sat down, I had noticed and smiled at a prominent placard hanging on the backbar: BUREAUCRACY IS A SYSTEM FOR CONVERTING ENERGY INTO SOLID WASTE. An aphorism to take home to my bureaucrat wife, who works for the Oregon Department of Environmental Quality. Her agency's regulation of woodstove emissions, septic tanks, and agricultural pollution has made it an object of considerable hostility in rural Oregon. Federal agencies,

> *Whether it's physical space we most value, or the informal sociability here, or a less frenetic pace of life, or the freedom to be different, or all of those, we have* room *here, room to shake and plump our feathers and feel all right.*

too, have been derided and vilified, especially for the limits they have placed on public-land logging and grazing during the last decade. Many who make or made their livings from the land have felt stepped on by what they see as an overpowering alliance between government and environmentalists in the cities and suburbs.

To some extent they have been. But the story of government, like that of landscape, is not one-sided. For all their inflexibility and torpid pace of action, regulatory and land management agencies play crucial roles in protecting the very fluffing room the people in the tavern that day, and all Oregonians, value so dearly. The space to stretch and be yourself is pretty well compromised if your drinking water is contaminated or particles in the air are giving you breathing problems. And many of Steve Terrill's photographs would look quite different, and not for the better, if Oregon in the course of the twentieth century had not acquired and protected as much state park land as it has, especially on the coast. The photographs would

also look different if, in 1973, the legislature hadn't passed the Oregon Land Use Act, which aims to balance conservation and development under the most comprehensive set of land-use planning principles ever adopted by any state. That the act and its implementation have not entirely pleased either devout preservationists or ardent developers strongly suggests that the act is working. Interest groups and legislators regularly seek to alter and amend it, which is fair enough—no law is good for all time as originally written—but we would be fools to weaken it much. It was and remains the most visionary public policy program of its kind in the country.

I broke out of such thoughts when the slippered bartender appeared with a new glass of beer—one I hadn't ordered. One of the men at the table had taken a seat at the bar. He smiled and touched the bill of his cap, which bore the logo of a heavy machinery company. "Passing through?" he asked.

"Passing through," I answered. I told him I'd once lived in Langell Valley, not far south. He knew a rancher there. Pretty country, we agreed, and our talk tailed off in pleasantries. I didn't tell him my main reason for visiting his part of the state, because I feared it would chill the friendliness of our encounter. I had stopped to see the Sycan River because I was writing the text for a coffee-table book about Oregon rivers protected by state and federal wild-and-scenic river designations. Among other angles, I was writing about the human uses and abuses of rivers that have made government protections necessary and may necessitate more.

I may have misjudged the man in the cap. He might not have been hostile to my views on rivers and their management. But the fact is that nature-preservation measures and those who promote them are bitterly resented, more bitterly than many in the urban centers of Oregon realize, in the rural reaches of the state. The placard about bureaucracy was a mild comment. A bumper sticker common in timber country is blunter: HELP OUR GOVERNMENT DESTROY AMERICA—JOIN AN ENVIRONMENTALIST CLUB. Environmentalists are seen as self-privileged outsiders who want the natural landscape set aside as a recreational playground and care nothing for those who live closer to the land and have traditionally worked the land, producing commodities the rest of us freely consume and take for granted. There is truth in their critique. And there is truth in the environmentalist critique that resource production has been too heavily favored above other uses of the land, that economy must be brought into balance with ecology, and that the public lands are the common property and responsibility of all Americans wherever they live.

Hostility has hardened the argument, and because of that prevailing climate I declined to tell a friendly inquirer what I was doing in his country. I feared what he might think of me—and, I suppose, what I might think of him—if our views and purposes had become known. I finished my beer and left the genial company of the tavern regretting my cowardice. The man in the cap and I might have disagreed about who should manage rivers and forests and how, but I had a feeling there was much we might have agreed on, too. We knew and felt a bond with the same landscape. We both loved it. If he and I and all those who care about Oregon's future could recognize and honor that love in each other, despite our differences, we might ease the tension and escape the polarized debate in which we've trapped ourselves. We might find there is work we can do together. We might find there is work we can only do together.

❖ ❖ ❖ ❖ ❖

MY FRIEND FRANK BOYDEN, a ceramist, printmaker, and Oregon native who lives at Cascade Head, has been known to stop at the border and do a little dance when returning home, he's so glad to live in this state. I'm not a native and not much of a dancer, but I know how he feels. I felt it on a sunny day in February 1995, near the end of a transcontinental drive, when I crossed the Snake River and left Idaho and I-84 for US 20 at Ontario. Oregon had been my home for many years, but on that trip, for the first time, I felt an elated sense of entering my own backyard. I steered my truck west in a happy trance.

The flat fields of the Snake River plain, just furzing up with something green, gave off the sour scent of last year's onions. On through Vale, following the Malheur River with its raw cutbanks, a few pintails floating the easy current. The low-lying hills turned from blue to sensuous brown as they gradually surrounded me, the highway weaving among them into higher country dotted with junipers and crops of dark volcanic rock—country that must have looked much the same a hundred years ago and a hundred years before that. A magpie flew from a shaggy fence post. Angus and Herefords, impassive behind barbed wire. Then Juntura, a tiny town at the confluence of two forks of the Malheur, a Bible church at one end of town, a little brick Catholic church at the other.

US 20 made its way higher again, past a white ranch house with a windbreak of leafless tall poplars, the hay put up in giant rolled bales. Drinkwater Pass, then Stinkingwater Pass—it might have been important not to confuse them a century ago—and I was in the northernmost reach of the Great Basin, crossing streams that never touch sea. The pavement shot dead straight for twenty miles across Pleistocene lake bed. A windmill, three graceful pintos. Steens Mountain in white solitude fifty miles south, called Snow Mountain on pioneer maps. In Burns I was shocked to find not one but two espresso shops, a McDonald's, and a little mall called Steens Mountain Plaza. I felt my usual ambivalence about progress—a pang of regret that even Burns was not immune, but the coffee, pretty good coffee, was warm in my hand and belly.

Westward out of town, the big country took on a subtle roll. Too early in the year for sage grouse to be strutting near Sagehen Summit, too early for the blue haze of camas in the swales near Riley. The highway angled right, northwest, in long looping winds, slowly rising and falling, passing snow-dusted Squaw Butte, Glass Butte, Round Top Butte. Tilted telephone poles ran alongside, keeping me company. To the north, a mottled cheatgrass sea turned rich with the evening sun. Three crows, a tan doublewide, and ahead on the western horizon, three tiny arrowhead tips—the Sisters? The tips dipped out of sight, popped up, dipped away, then rose in full relief. The Sisters for sure, blue against the saffron sky, Broken Top to their south. On through the eye-blink town of Brothers, named by lonely sheepherders watching the regal Sisters from three little bumps in the desert, and on through dusk and darkness into Bend.

In the morning I escaped as quickly as I could the congestion of Oregon's Recreationville. It's always been a crossroads—pioneers forded the Deschutes River here, at a double-curve called Farewell Bend—but the traffic is a mite thicker now. The highway led me north of northwest, past new manufactured homes on plots of sagebrush flat. The Sisters, huge, off the truck's port bow—the two who like to talk to each other, the third who keeps to herself. Washington, a pinhead on square shoulders; Three-Fingered Jack, missing at least two fingers; Jefferson, classic and fat with snow; and Hood hunkered far to the north. Landmarks to Native Americans, to pioneers, to Oregonians today. Some western states have clutters of peaks. Ours are few and singular.

Junipers gave way to ponderosas as the truck climbed the grade, the first tall trees I'd seen since…well, since leaving Oregon two months before. Then Douglas firs and true firs, Santiam Pass, south on 126. Bright water spilling from mossy roadside cliffs, the truck running easily, like a horse that just sniffed home. Down and down through a continuous canyon of tall, wet-barked trees, each in its own littered snow well, dirty snow mounded along the shoulder. The McKenzie River flashed into view on my left. From Blue River on, the mountain slopes displayed their bad haircuts. I hit the flats at Leaburg—fruit trees blooming pink and white, sheep and llamas in the pastures, surely the greenest green grass in all the world. And with the green, inevitably, the weather that makes it so. I'd had clear sailing all three days from Chicago, 2,000 miles of winter sun, and now? My dear gray Willamette Valley, sprinkling rain.

I skirted the north side of Eugene and rolled on west, passing a heron holding still in a marshy backwater of the Long Tom River, my watershed. The flat pastureland merged ahead into the misted Coast Range hills, the road steering itself and me through familiar curves and straightaways. One last straight, one last curve, and I turned into the home acre. I gave the truck a pat on the dashboard, switched it off, and clambered out stiff from the drive. The trees were right where I'd left them. As always, they lifted my gaze to their pointed crowns, more than a hundred feet high. The biggest were seedlings when Benjamin Gifford began taking his pictures of Oregon. They'll be a stand of old growth, we hope, when someone takes pictures a century from now. Before entering the house, I circled the place in a slow walk, listening to the little creek's lively song, breathing air moist and sweet with the scent of soil—that darkness, that rich mystery from which ferns and forest and even words sometimes, like these, will find their way.

ISBN 1-56579-380-3

Contemporary photography copyright: Steve Terrill, 2000.
    All rights reserved.
Historical text copyright: Thomas Robinson, 2000.
    All rights reserved.
Afterword copyright: John Daniel, 2000. All rights reserved.

Editor: Kelly Anton
Designer: Mark Mulvany
Production Manager: Craig Keyzer

Published by:
Westcliffe Publishers, Inc.
P.O. Box 1261
Englewood, CO 80150
www.westcliffepublishers.com

Printed in Hong Kong by C&C Offset Printing Co., Ltd.

Library of Congress Cataloging-in-Publication Data
Gifford, Benjamin A.
    Oregon : then & now / historical landscape photography by Benjamin Gifford; contemporary rephotography by Steve Terrill ; historical essay by Thomas Robinson ; afterword by John Daniel.
        p. cm.
    Includes bibliographical references.
    ISBN 1-56579-380-3
    1. Oregon--History--Pictorial works. 2. Oregon--Pictorial works. 3. Landscape--Oregon--Pictorial works. 4. Oregon--Description and travel. I. Title: Oregon then & now. II. Terrill, Steve. III. Robinson, Thomas, 1952- IV. Title.

F877 .G54 2000
979.5--dc21

00-040854

*For more information about other fine books and calendars from Westcliffe Publishers, please contact your local bookstore, call us at 1-800-523-3692, write for our free color catalog, or visit us on the Web at **www.westcliffepublishers.com**.*

ABOUT THE PHOTOGRAPHER

Steve Terrill, a self-taught photographer, is a native of Portland, Oregon. His works are included in Oregon tourism publications and numerous books, calendars, and magazines from publishers such as *National Geographic Publications, Sierra Club, Travel & Leisure,* and *Readers' Digest.* Terrill has published twelve photography books, including five through Westcliffe Publishers including *Oregon Coast, Wildflowers of Oregon,* and *Oregon Reflections.*

ABOUT THE AUTHORS

Thomas Robinson is a photograph archivist, conservator, and historian who does darkroom printing, research, and conservation work for fine art photographers, museums, and archives. He is the author of *Oregon Photographers: 1852–1917* and other publications about the history of photography. Robinson, 47, has lived in Portland, Oregon, for the last twenty-five years.

John Daniel, a poet, essayist, and writer of memoirs, lives near the Long Tom River north of Noti, Oregon. He is the author of six books, including *Oregon Rivers*, a collaboration with photographer Larry N. Olson, published by Westcliffe in 1997. Daniel teaches creative writing in conferences and writer-in-residence positions around the country.

BIBLIOGRAPHY

Benjamin Gifford's Biographical Information: Books
Ballou, Robert. *Early Klickitat Valley Days.* Goldendale, Washington: Goldendale Sentinel, 1938.
Brown, Robert O. *Nineteenth Century Portland, Oregon Photographers.* Portland, Oregon: author, 1991.
Culp, Edwin D. *Yesterday in Oregon.* Caldwell, Idaho: Caxton, 1992.
McNeal, William Howard. *History of Wasco County, Oregon.* The Dalles, Oregon: author, 1953, revised edition 1974.
Oregon State University Archives, copies of Gifford family scrapbook.
Pictorial Oregon. Portland, Oregon: Portland Press Club, 1915.
Robinson, Thomas. *Oregon Photographers: 1852–1917.* Portland, Oregon: author, second edition, 1993.

Benjamin Gifford's Biographical Information: Periodicals
NOTE: Many of the following newspaper articles are included in the Gifford family scrapbook and were reprinted in full in the book, Oregon Photographers: 1852–1917.
Better Fruit, Hood River, Oregon: 1906.
The Dalles Weekly Chronicle, 1902–1910.
Oregon Journal, August 28, 1929.
Oregonian, 1891–1893.
Oregonian, 5, May 26, 1946.
Oregonian, 7, March 6, 1936.
Oregon Journal, Vol. 8, March 6, 1936.
Pacific Monthly, through 1910.
Sunset magazine, through 1915.
The Dalles Optimist, October 18, 1962.
Reed, S. G. *Neahkahnie Mountain.* Portland: S. G. Reed, 1910.

Books Illustrated by Benjamin Gifford
Gifford, Benjamin A. *Art Works of Portland, Mt. Hood and The Columbia River.* Oshkosh, Wisconsin: Art Photogravure Co., 1913.
Gifford, Benjamin A. *Art Works of the State of Oregon.* Oshkosh, Wisconsin: Art Photogravure Co., 1909.
Gifford, Benjamin A. *Snapshots on the Columbia.* The Dalles, Oregon: author, 1902.

Information about Photographic Processes and History
Hasluck, Paul N. *The Book of Photography.* London and New York: Cassell, 1907.
Jenkins, Resse V. *Images & Enterprise.* Baltimore, Maryland, and London: The John Hopkins University Press, 1975.
Munson, Doug. "Gelatine Chloride Printing Out Paper" pamphlet. Housatonic, Massachusetts: Chicago Albumen Works, ca. 1997.

Rephotographic Survey Work
Klett, Mark, et al. *Second View, The Rephotographic Survey Project.* Albuquerque: University of New Mexico, 1984.

Afterword Sources
Ambrose, Stephen E. *Undaunted Courage: Meriwether Lewis, Thomas Jefferson, and the Opening of the American West.* New York: Simon & Schuster, 1996.
McArthur, Lewis A. *Oregon Geographic Names.* Sixth edition, revised and enlarged by Lewis L. McArthur. Portland, Oregon: Oregon Historical Society Press, 1992.
O'Donnell, Terence. "Oregon History." In *Oregon Blue Book 1999–2000.* Salem, Oregon: Office of the Secretary of State, 1999.
Orr, Elizabeth L., William N. Orr, and Ewart M. Baldwin. *Geology of Oregon,* fourth edition. Dubuque, Iowa: Kendall/Hunt, 1992.
Robbins, William G. *Landscapes of Promise: The Oregon Story, 1800–1940.* Seattle: University of Washington, 1997.
Taylor, George H., and Chris Hannan. *The Climate of Oregon: From Rain Forest to Desert.* Corvallis: Oregon State University, 1999.

ACKNOWLEDGMENTS

Thomas Robinson made the POP prints from Gifford's original negatives in the Oregon Historical Society, and Jenny Ankeny performed the gold toning and processing. The two, Robinson and Ankeny, also made the black & white prints of Steve Terrill's negatives. Robinson and Evan Schneider shot the color copy photography of Gifford's original prints, postcards, and ephemera. Steve Terrill thanks Larry Geddis, Jeff Gregor, Laurie Hicks, Georjean Melonas, Bob Reiter, Bill Wolfe, Scott Wolfe, and everyone else who graciously granted him access to their property and directed him to many locations. He extends a special thank-you to his son, Steve, who accompanied him and assisted him with the rephotography. PhotoCraft processed Steve Terrill's black & white negatives and all color copy transparencies. John Laursen reviewed John Daniel's Afterword with a discerning eye, for which we thank him.

Photo Sources: Oregon Historical Society, Norma Eid, Michael Fairley, Steve Kenney, Kathryn McElwee, Norm Moore, Karen Runkel, and Terry Toedtemeier.

In addition to those who provided photographs, we thank the following individuals for their valuable assistance in providing information: Garth Ankeny, Paul Bassett, Robert Brown, Mona Campbell, Joslyn Howells, Linda Jerofke, Steve Kenney, Larry Landis, and James H. Raley.

The staff of the Oregon Historical Society, who acted above and beyond the call of duty to enhance the quality of this project, are Elizabeth Anderson, Sharon Howe, Richard Jost, Evan Schneider, Susan Seyl, Melinda Simms, Amanda Tillstrom, Mikki Tint, and Elizabeth Winroth.

HISTORIC PHOTO CREDITS

The historic photos in this book, all taken by Benjamin Gifford, were provided by the following sources. The photo numbers prefixed OHS or CN are from the Oregon Historical Society; all others were provided by individual donors.

Page#	Photo Credit	Page#	Photo Credit	Page#	Photo Credit	Page#	Photo Credit
Preface		44	OHS Gi 4833	96	Thomas Robinson	140	OHS Gi 307
4	Mike Fairley	46	OHS Gi 4525	97	Norma Eid	142	OHS Gi 569
		48	OHS Gi 1152	98	OHS Gi 6510A	144	OHS Gi 851
Biography		50	OHS Gi 6443	100	OHS 4127A	146	OHS Gi 1827
5	Thomas Robinson	51	OHS Gi 5508	102	OHS Gi 821	148	OHS Gi 582
6	OrHi 63826A	52	OHS Gi 2526	103	OHS Gi 7699	150	OHS Gi 305.5
8	Anonymous donor	54	OHS Gi 5177	104	OHS Gi 7894	152	OHS Gi 301.5
9	Anonymous donor	56	OHS Gi 2770	106	OHS Gi 8616	154	OHS Gi 6836
10	OrHi 61472A	57	Karen Runkel	108	Steve Kenney	156	OHS Gi 606
11	CN 023379A	58	OHS Gi 10451	109	OHS Gi 1128	158	OHS Gi 1618
12	OrHi 1105			110	OHS Gi 787	160	Karen Runkel
13	OrHi 101536	**Willamette Valley**		112	OHS Gi 1098	161	OHS Gi 8307
14	OHS Gi 8813	60	OHS Gi 1732	114	OHS Gi 8045		
		62	OHS Gi 7789A	116	OHS Gi 210	**Southern Oregon**	
Oregon Coast		64	OHS Gi 682	117	OHS Gi 329	164	OHS Gi C5
16	OHS OrHi 7865	65	OHS Gi 687	118	OHS Gi 187	166	OHS Gi C7
18	OHS Gi 1654	66	OHS Gi 2501	120	OHS Gi 563	167	OHS Gi C14
19	OHS Gi 1657	68	OHS Gi 679	121	OHS Gi 189	168	OHS Gi 1053
20	OHS Gi 7765	70	OHS Gi 3478	122	OHS Gi 4431	170	OHS Gi 1055
22	Karen Runkel	71	OHS Gi 516			172	OHS Gi 1918
24	OHS Gi 1885	72	OHS Gi 6729	**Cascades and Eastern**		174	Karen Runkel
26	OHS Gi 388	74	OHS Gi 489	**Oregon**		176	Karen Runkel
28	OHS Gi 389	76	OHS Gi 493	124	Thomas Robinson	178	OHS Gi 1915
29	OHS Gi 7258	78	OHS Gi 486	126	Steve Kenney	180	OHS Gi 1888
30	OHS Gi 514	79	OHS Gi 425	127	Steve Kenney	181	OHS Gi 1922
31	OHS Gi 1362	80	OHS Gi 1903	128	Steve Kenney	182	Karen Runkel
32	OHS Gi 7266			130	Steve Kenney	184	OHS Gi 1913
34	OHS Gi 6387	**Columbia River Gorge**		132	OHS Gi 604 (left);	186	OHS Gi 1280
36	OHS Gi 6407	82	OHS Gi 338		OHS Gi 538		
37	OHS Gi 13026	83	OHS Gi 5848.5	133	OHS Gi 277		
		84	Thomas Robinson	134	OHS Gi 279		
Portland		86	Norm Moore	135	OHS Gi 4016 (left);		
38	OHS Gi 2542	88	OHS Gi 5838		OHS Gi 4015		
40	OHS Gi 4856	90	OHS Gi 5852	136	OHS Gi 349		
41	Steve Terrill	92	OHS Gi 6232	137	OHS Gi 350		
42	OHS Gi 5910	94	OHS Gi 7338	138	OHS Gi 339